Scar 2.0: Family Scars Run Deep

Producer Larry Love

Published by Producer Larry Love, 2025.

SCAR 2.0:
Family Scars Run Deep

To Crime/Thriller Lovers
Creator: Producer Larry Love
First published in the USA in 2025
Copyrighted Material 2024
The moral rights of the author has been asserted
Star Blaze Productions, Miami, Florida
ISBN: 979-8-9927229-1-8
thescar2.com

Table of Contents

Chapter 1
A Son's Farewell

In a parallel universe in a city called McCall, Idaho, a solemn casket hole waits in silence. The polished casket is poised above it, ready for its final descent. Tomas Montgomery stands among his family, their faces marked with grief as they gather to say goodbye to Elizabeth Montgomery, beloved mother and community figure.

Tomas sits, shoulders heavy, surrounded by the mourning family as the priest's voice rises, delivering the eulogy with heartfelt reverence.

"As we acknowledge this day as a day of sadness, I know Elizabeth would want us to have a smile on our faces. She gave to this community religiously. She made her church family her family, and she raised her son with the vigilance that a mother who loves her son would. She left footprints for us to follow—not footprints that are easily washed away, but footprints embedded in our hearts to be carried forever. It's God's love that has wrapped Elizabeth with everlasting wings. For it's the power of Christ that will keep her safe and cherished, carried and kept by the promises of God. Now unto Him, which is able to keep us from falling, hold this family up in their time of despair."

The priest's words hang in the air as Tomas rises quietly, helping an elderly lady beside him toward the limo waiting nearby. Her tearful eyes search his face as she clasps his arm.

"She was the world to me. She helped me so much when my husband died. I don't know what I'm going to do without her. She was such a gem."

"Yes, she was," he replies softly, each word weighted with his own sorrow. He glances over to see a young woman standing nearby, talking to another. Tomas gestures, drawing her attention.

"Crystal, can you escort Ms. Mary to the limo?"

"Sure, I can. You ready, Miss Mary?"

"Yes, honey."

The elderly lady turns to Tomas, her voice tender with concern. "You're not going back with us?"

"There's something I have to take care of," Tomas says gently. "Crystal has you."

"Okay." She gives him a lingering look, her hand patting his gently before Crystal leads her away. Tomas watches them move toward the limo before his gaze shifts across the lot. In the distance, a black SUV waits. His best friend, Hector, leans against it, arms folded, eyes fixed on Tomas.

As Tomas approaches, stepping closer, Tomas expression grows resolute. "Let's do this."

Hector's face breaks into a faint smile, one filled with understanding. He nods, slipping into the driver's seat as Tomas gets in beside him.

"That's what I like to hear."

As they drive off, Tomas's gaze flickers to the rearview mirror, catching sight of the men at the graveside as they begin to lower his mother's casket. A whisper falls from his lips, barely audible.

"Sorry, Mom, I have to do this."

The SUV glides down the winding path, carrying Tomas away from the funeral grounds and toward an uncertain future.

Chapter 2
Tomas Meets D.J.

The plane descended toward Miami International Airport, its shadow tracing the coastline below. Tomas and Hector stepped out of the terminal, suitcases in hand, and loaded them into an SUV waiting at the curb. Climbing in, they settled back as the Uber pulled away, merging into the city's lively flow. As they drove, Miami's vibrant sights passed by in a colorful blur—palm trees swaying and the bright shimmer of the water in the distance.

Soon, the SUV turned into an upscale neighborhood where mansions stood behind high gates and manicured lawns. The driver spoke briefly into the intercom by the gate, which then slid open, granting them entry. The SUV rolled up a long driveway, revealing a sprawling estate guarded by men stationed strategically around the grounds. Tomas and Hector exchanged a glance, taking in the scale of the place.

At the entrance, they climbed out of the SUV, and the driver handed over their suitcases before driving off. They approached the grand doors, which opened to reveal a maid waiting inside with a welcoming smile.

"Hello, Mr. Montgomer." she greeted. "Can you and your friend please leave your bags here? We'll have someone bring them in. And please, follow me."

The maid stepped outside and closed the door. She had Tomas and Hector follow her around the enormous and alluring mansion, where a vast pool area spread out before them. They paused for a moment, in awe of the scene—a group of beautiful women in bikinis lounged by the pool, exchanging smiles with them as they entered. Hector nudged Tomas, nodding toward the women.

"With the victor comes the spoils." he murmured, grinning.

At the cabana by the pool, the sound of a loud voice called out to them.

"Tomas! Toma! You finally made it!"

They turned to see a man approaching with open arms. He clasped Tomas's hand warmly.

"I'm glad you're here. I'm sorry to hear about your mom. So sorry. I've been there. But I'm here to help you with this new chapter of life."

He looked at Hector.

"And who is this?"

"D.J., this is my friend and partner, Hector."

D.J. extended his hand with a welcoming smile, and Hector shook it, nodding in appreciation.

"Well, Mr. Hector, I welcome you to this new chapter we're about to establish."

"Thank you, Mr. D.J. You have a beautiful home."

"Okay, I called you 'Mr.,' you called me 'Mr.' Now let's get rid of the formalities. Call me D.J."

"D.J. it is then."

"I don't know if he told you," he began glancing between Tomas and Hector, "but Tomas's family is the foundation of what my family built. I'm glad he's finally come so we can honor that properly."

"I thank you for the invitation," Tomas replied, his tone sincere. "I realize the power of working together."

He led them back to the bar, giving Hector a knowing look.

"His father and my father were business partners. His father even saved my father's life."

He paused, a faint smile crossing his face as if recalling a distant memory.

"My father told me the family story, told me that they were a tight cord. My father was indebted to Tomas's father until his dying breath. And that loyalty was tested, too."

Reaching into a small fridge, he pulled out a vase of mojitos, cold condensation beading on the glass.

"Please, taste my mojitos. I'm a master at making these."

He poured the drinks, handing each man a glass.

"Because of your father, he got to live another day to raise his family. Big on family, my father realized that."

He paused, looking at each of them in turn.

"I don't believe that ended when they died. I believe it can continue with their bloodline. That's why I didn't come talking about some job, but I came talking about partnership."

"A partnership?" Tomas echoed, casting a quick glance at Hector before looking back. "I know when we talked over the phone, you said if I came, you were offering me an opportunity. But a partnership?"

"Yes. Your father shared the blueprint of expansion of distribution. That's what my father started to share with me before he died."

He gestured around, his voice brimming with pride.

"I pieced those things together, studied their history, refined what they built, made it stronger. Better."

Tomas took a sip, then raised an eyebrow.

"What makes it better?"

Sipping his drink, D.J. studied Tomas and Hector with a slow, thoughtful smile. He set his glass down.

"Let me show you. Follow me. Take your drinks."

Leaving the cabana, they trailed after him as he addressed the women by the pool with a grin.

"Ladies, we'll be back. Make sure you leave the water wet for us."

The women giggled as they continued to the back entrance of the mansion.

"Beautiful, huh?" He said, gesturing to the expanse of the property. "I understand our fathers' flaws. I know better. It takes an assortment of people and organism. I understand."

He opened the grand back entrance, revealing the opulent interior.

"Greatness isn't achieved alone."

Tomas and Hector took in the view, their eyes widening as they stepped inside. The entry hall was vast, with two sweeping staircases leading up to the main office. The walls were painted a pristine white with gleaming gold fixtures, and in the center stood a five-foot marble statue of two arms intertwined, hands clasped in unity.

He walked over to the statue and placed a hand on it.

"Here, we do it together."

"This is amazing." Tomas murmured, marveling at the space.

"Yes," D.J. continued.

He pointed to the statue.

"One hand washes the other, the left not knowing what the right is doing, but they must come together to clean itself."

He climbed the staircase quickly, Tomas and Hector following close behind.

"Set your eyes on this."

At the top, he reached the double doors of the main office and pushed them open.

"Welcome to Brain Central."

They stepped inside to see a vast office with polished gold fixtures and walls embedded with dark reddish-brown marble. A stylish wooden desk commanded the center, while marble statues and an extensive book collection lined one wall, adding a sense of timeless opulence to the space.

Tomas looked around, impressed.

"I see you're what they call state-of-the-art."

"This is where all the mental business gets done," He said, gesturing around the grand office. "Never bring anything illegal or big money to where you lay your head. If Homeland comes, they get nothing."

He tapped the bookshelf behind his desk, his expression unreadable.

"I made some modifications in case hell ever decides to come knocking. Hell doesn't want to see what I got behind this bookcase."

Moving to the set of double French doors on the left side of the office, he opened them wide, stepping onto the balcony with a satisfied smile as he gazed down at the women by the pool.

"Lesson: never have your back compromised. Always see who's coming."

Tomas and Hector joined him on the balcony, taking in the view.

"You seem like you're ready." Tomas remarked.

Hector grinned, catching the attention of one of the women and waving.

D.J. nodded, turning his attention back to them.

"I also made some modifications outside the office. Let's just say you don't want to be on the wrong side of that door."

Tomas chuckled, giving a nod of approval.

"I feel safer than being in the White House."

A hearty laugh burst from D.J.

"Ha, ha! Yes!"

All three shared a laugh. Turning serious, D.J. looked at Tomas.

"Before I show you more, is this something you can partner with? As you see, I'm committed."

"We didn't come all the way here to turn back," Tomas replied. "There's no reverse on our gears."

A grin spread across his face.

"That's what I like to hear. Let's see where this partnership takes us. But first, let's party. Did you bring changing clothes?"

"Yes, we did."

"Perfect. You can take a couple of the guest rooms, change, and then we'll take these ladies on a night on the town."

With that, he beckoned to the women by the pool.

"Señoritas!"

Chapter 3
Club Decision

Music pounds through the air, pulsing in time with the energy of Miami's vibrant club scene. Overhead, the city skyline glows against the night sky, framing the flashing lights below. Inside, beautiful women dance atop the bar. Bottle girls weave through the crowd with glittering bottles, and people move in rhythm, lost in the night. A famous athlete catches a moment of attention in the VIP area before blending back into the scene.

Hector dances with a stunning woman, and next to him, Tomas is moving with another. Hector leans in close, his voice just audible over the music.

"There's nothing like this in Idaho. I could get used to this quickly."

Tomas, keeping his eyes on the scene, doesn't miss a beat.

"Never get relaxed, even when you're having a good time. This is a different jungle. Miami it has exotic creatures."

The woman with Tomas leans back, dancing against him and locking eyes, her smile sly.

"This is the kind of exotic creature I want roaming around my house," Hector jokes, grinning at the women around him.

They grin back, clearly enjoying the banter. Tomas laughs.

"Let me roam to the bar for a drink. You just make sure you got your shots, you rabies-sick fuck."

Hector laughs, shaking his head as Tomas takes his dancing partner's hand and leads her toward the bar.

At the bar, D.J. stands with two women, chatting and laughing over drinks. Tomas sits down next to him, his arm around his own dance partner as he signals to the bartender.

"Let me get two rum and Cokes."

D.J. catches sight of Tomas and slaps his shoulder.

"Are you having a good time or what, huh?"

Tomas nods, taking in the scene.

"Yes. Quite impressive."

D.J. grins. "This is one of many more to come. I just wanted to get your beak wet. When you get your drink, come meet me on the VIP balcony."

He gestures to the VIP section, then saunters off toward the balcony. Tomas watches him go before turning back to his drink.

In the VIP balcony, D.J. lights a cigar, taking a long draw as security ushers the last few people back into the main club. Tomas enters, moving over to join him. D.J. gestures to the spacious balcony, a hint of pride in his voice.

"This is one of the biggest clubs in Miami, and I can section off a part of it just to talk to you. Do you know why?"

"You're the boss," Tomas replies.

"That's right. I paid the cost to be the boss. I paid my dues. Your father understood that. He became the man by putting in the work. He spilled blood—a bloodbath. I've spilled blood. Have you spilled blood?"

"Are you asking if I've killed someone?" Tomas replies.

D.J. meets Tomas's gaze, his stare intense. Tomas hesitates.

"Hector is the one that put that type of work in Idaho."

D.J. doesn't break eye contact.

"To go down this road, blood must be on your hands. I can't have a partner that I don't know he won't get down if I need him to."

He pauses, letting the weight of his words sink in.

"I need you to take care of a problem for me. It's a test. I'm not hiding that from you."

"What's the problem?"

D.J. takes another puff, the smoke curling between them.

"This is a personal situation. By my niece's school, there's a guy who sells to the students. A big no-no. A local dick. He was already given a warning. He left but found his way back to selling to the children again. This can't be tolerated. You understand?"

Tomas nods, holding D.J.'s gaze.

"If you are the man to take care of this problem, I need you to do it in a specific way. No guns. A gun lets you keep your distance with the kill. This kill must be up close and personal, either with a knife or with your bare hands."

Tomas looks at D.J., taking in the weight of the ask.

"No pressure. If you can't do this, he'll be dead by the end of the week regardless. But if you don't do it, we'll continue having a good night, realize this ain't for you, and go our separate ways."

Tomas considers the proposition, searching D.J.'s expression for any sign of hesitation, but D.J.'s face remains calm, his gaze unwavering. After a beat, Tomas looks at him.

"Where's your niece's school?"

A slow smirk spreads across D.J.'s face.

"We'll do it two days from now. I'll send my guy Carlos with you. Tomorrow you can scout the location. He'll have all the particulars."

D.J. extends his hand, and Tomas grips it firmly.

D.J. says, "Like father, like son".

Chapter 4

The Tomas Test

The following Monday, around after-school time, Carlos drives Tomas and Hector to the pizzeria where the drug dealer sells pills to students. Slowly, they approach the back where they have a good view of the dealer, posted by the large green and blue dumpsters behind the store.

"Just like D.J. said, students head to the back of the store where transactions are quietly taking place. This is where he's posted," Carlos explains. "D.J. wanted you to see what he's doing. We don't sell to kids—that puta. What are you going to do?"

Tomas stares silently, observing the dealer's every move.

"Is that where he's posted every day?"

"Yeah. He gets there about 15 minutes before the kids get out of school."

Hector frowns, thinking. "How are you going to get close? He's going to be suspicious seeing a new guy approach him."

Tomas rubs his chin, watching and considering each angle.

"So you said he gets there 15 minutes before the kids let out?"

"Yes."

"All right, we'll get there 30 minutes before him. I'll hide in one of those dumpsters. Hector, I need you to call him by the dumpster like you want to buy something. I'll handle it from there."

Turning to Carlos, Tomas nods.

"Carlos, you post here so you can watch what's going down and have the car ready to get us out of here. We'll do it tomorrow."

Carlos nods. "Okay. We only got six, seven minutes tops."

"Don't worry. It'll be smooth and easy," Tomas replies.

Carlos slowly drives off.

The next day at 1:30 PM, they return to the same spot. The alley is empty. No dealer, no students around yet. After 15 minutes, Tomas turns to Hector.

"Let's do this."

Tomas gets out of the car, walks up to the dumpsters, and chooses one that seems suitable. He signals to Hector that this is the one, then jumps in and closes the lid. Inside, he pulls out a knife and cracks the lid just enough to see the drug dealer approaching, right on schedule.

At 2:15, the dealer arrives. He posts up by another dumpster, waiting for the students to be released. Hector steps out of the car, dressed in tattered clothes, and walks toward the back area. He whistles, catching the dealer's attention.

The dealer, unfamiliar with Hector, waves him off. Hector calls out again, persistent, but the dealer isn't interested—until Hector pulls out a wad of cash. That does the trick.

The dealer starts walking over. Hector moves slowly toward Tomas's dumpster, positioning himself so the dealer's back is to it.

"What do you want?" the dealer grunts.

"My cousin at the school said you got that stack. You see I got the bread. Might buy your whole stash before the kids get out. Let me see what you got."

The dealer eyes Hector suspiciously but, lured by the cash, rationalizes that it's a good deal. He turns sideways, reaching into his pocket.

"I can get out of here early today. I got some perks and molly, and I also—"

Suddenly, he notices the dumpster lid is cracked, as if someone is watching him.

"What the fuck?"

In that split second, Tomas springs the lid open and lunges, aiming to stab, but the dealer reacts fast. Grabbing Tomas's arm, the knife falls. A struggle breaks out, and the dealer tosses Tomas out of the dumpster, both landing hard on the ground.

Hector, watching the fight, keeps his distance, knowing Tomas has to handle this himself.

The dealer reaches for a gun tucked behind his jacket. Tomas, seeing the motion, slams him against the dumpster, causing the gun to fall. They grapple, fists swinging, but the dealer gains the upper hand.

Carlos, watching from the car, realizes the situation is dire. He steps out and approaches the alley fast but discreetly. Hector reaches for his gun, ready to step in, but Carlos stops him, signaling that Tomas has to do this alone. Hector nods, though reluctantly.

Tomas, now straining against the dealer, manages to get behind him, locking him in a chokehold and wrapping his legs around the dealer's waist. The dealer desperately reaches for the gun, but it's out of reach. Tomas notices his knife nearby.

He grabs it and, with three quick strikes to the dealer's chest, feels the drug dealer's strength fade from him. Breathless, Tomas looks down, staring at his bloodied hands. He pushes the lifeless dealer off of him.

Hector moves quickly, pulling Tomas to his feet, and Carlos drags the dealer's body to the side of the dumpster, hiding it from view.

"Let's go, amigo. You did it." Hector says.

They rush back to the car and drive off. As they speed away, a lone student appears in the alley, wanting drugs, scanning the empty space where the dealer once stood.

Chapter 5

New Beginnings

Later that evening, Carlos pulls up with Tomas and Hector at the Rickenbacker Causeway bridge, overlooking the Miami skyline. Carlos parks the car, stepping out to smoke a cigarette. Tomas follows him, glancing at the horizon before speaking up.

"How long do we have to wait?" Tomas asks, his tone laced with impatience.

"Stop being paranoid. It's done. They're coming," Carlos replies, dismissing his concerns with a wave of his hand.

"Don't tell me not to be paranoid. We still got the murder weapon on us, and I probably still have some of this guy's DNA on me," Tomas insists, his anxiety evident.

"If you did what I told you to do, you have no trace on you," Carlos counters, trying to reassure him.

Tomas walks over to the window where Hector is sitting.

"Hand me the duffle bag with the clothes and knife so I can dump it."

Hector grabs the duffle bag, gets out of the car, and hands it to Tomas.

"My man had it in him. There were no worries. I had your back if it didn't go your way."

Tomas jumps over the small barrier toward the river to get rid of the duffle bag.

Carlos addresses Hector.

"You would've messed it up for everybody if you interfered. I'm glad I was there to stop you."

"Hey! I was in control. I knew the rules." "You knew the rules?"

"You had your hand on your gun! What the fuck you talking about!" "Cabrón! You think I was going to leave there without my man?" "We were there to see if Tomas had the balls."

Hector confronts Carlos more sternly.

"There's no chickens on this team."

Carlos pauses and looks Hector up and down.

"Looks like Tomas wasn't the only one trying to prove himself today, huh? You got the big cojones, Hector. You look weighted down over there."

Carlos sees a Land Rover appear. Carlos starts to giggle.

"Relax."

Tomas jumps back over the barrier and walks back to the car. The Land Rover parks behind the car, and Carlos walks over to it.

Three men get out of the Land Rover. Two of the men look like they're security, scanning the area, while the third man goes to the back of the Land Rover and pulls out a large duffle bag. He walks over to Carlos's trunk as Carlos opens it. The man with the duffle bag puts it in Carlos' trunk, hands Carlos a piece of paper, and walks back to the Land Rover. Carlos closes the trunk.

Tomas and Hector approach Carlos at the back of the car.

"You fulfilled your side. D.J. wants to show his appreciation. This bag will set you up."

Carlos hands Tomas the paper.

"D.J. wants to meet with you at the location on the paper. It's formal. What's in the bag, make sure you buy some nice suits for the meet."

Carlos tosses Tomas the car keys.

"I'm going with them. Get rid of the car."

"Hey, Tomas, the DNA might be off you, but the blood is still on your hands. Good job, señor."

Carlos walks over to the Land Rover, gets inside, and it drives off.

Tomas and Hector watch as it disappears down the road. Hector takes the keys from Tomas and opens the trunk. He unzips the duffle bag.

"Whoa!"

Tomas looks inside the duffle bag as well, and they both see bundles of bricks of money alongside guns.

"We're set up, man. We can now party like rock stars," Tomas says.

"This is not party money," Hector replies.

"What are you talking about? Miami hasn't seen partying like what we're about to do," Tomas retorts.

"You know why money has a face on it? To let you know who rules, even when they're dead and gone. And whoever holds their faces has a voice. No money, no voice. D.J. just gave us a voice tonight."

As Tomas looks up at the high rises of the Miami skyline, Hector looks at the money and nods in agreement.

"We're one step closer to the American dream. Zip it up, and let's get rid of the car."

Hector closes the trunk. They both get in the car and drive off.

Chapter 6
Belly of the Beast

Another day in Little Haiti, a mom-and-pop store sits on a quiet corner. Suddenly, two black party vans with dark-tinted windows pull up to the sidewalk. The doors swing open, and 40 imposing black men step out, taking positions outside the store. Moments later, a sleek Maybach SUV pulls up. The driver steps out and walks to the back door, while the front passenger door opens, revealing an intimidating man known as Mr. Grande.

The driver opens the back door, and a black man with a fur coat, named Deamonotay, emerges. A young man with a folder approaches Deamonotay .

"Brother, what's the update?" Deamonotay asks.

Deamonotay, his brother Daniel, Mr. Grande, and the driver make their way into the store.

"He still hasn't signed," Daniel responds. "So we prepped him. All the minority landowners have complied. After this guy, we need to focus on the majority owner, which is D.J."

Deamonotay nods thoughtfully. "We don't have any leverage, even with all the minority land contracts. It shows that we're serious about our plans, that can begin to start the conversation with D.J."

"Fuck D.J.," Daniel says harshly. "We'll take that motherfucker like we're about to take it from this guy."

"You're talking about the biggest pill distributor in the southeastern region, and growing by the minute," Deamonotay cautions. "You can't take something from him without there being a disruption. It'll be better if we make him feel like he's giving it to us."

They make their way to the freezer area. Deamonotay takes off his fur coat, handing it to the driver, while Mr. Grande hands over his jacket as well. Both Deamonotay and Mr. Grande begin putting on freezer attire—boots, headgear, and gloves.

"'Give it to us?'" Daniel sneers. "What kind of psych class are you teaching? He's strong, but we have to show we've got a strong hand too."

With a smirk, Daniel presses a button, and a hidden door opens in the freezer. Deamonotay glances at the opening.

"Just like this secret room, domination doesn't need to be seen. That's ego."

Deamonotay, his brother Daniel, and Mr. Grande step through the secret door into a large, dimly lit room. In the center, a man lies strapped face down on a cold metal slab, completely naked. Metal hooks dangle from the ceiling, suspending a large hog above him, while a pool stick rests ominously against the wall in front of this exposed man's line of sight.

Deamonotay surveys the unsettling scene, a smirk playing at the corners of his mouth.

He says, "The plot thickens as we control the narrative,". His tone edged with menace.

He approaches the restrained man, pulls a chair close, and settles in beside him with unsettling calmness he begins.

"Mr. Torres, I heard you're having difficulties understanding the generous offer we've presented for your property."

Mr. Torres's eyes blaze with defiance.

"Fuck you, you son of a bitch! You think bringing me to this room is going to make me sign?"

Deamonotay chuckles softly.

"We understand the land you possess quite well, but it seems you've miscalculated what we are in possession of."

He raises a hand, signaling Daniel forward.

"Please, Daniel, elaborate for this distinguished gentleman."

With a smirk, Daniel steps closer.

"You are laid out in what we call the belly of the beast. See, we bring people here who might need to see our perspective a little more clearly."

Deamonotay leans in, both men casting glances toward the pool stick against the wall.

"Please bear with us," he murmurs, his tone darkening. "As we present our case to you more in-depth."

Deamonotay's laughter fills the room, echoing off the frigid metal walls. Rising, he walks over to the pool stick, gripping it tightly as he approaches Mr. Torres, whose defiant gaze falters at the sight of what's coming. Deamonotay leans forward slightly. His eyes locked on to Mr. Torres.

"There are many persuasive ways that we use to get the answer we're looking for. But I believe if you're going to be persuasive, then be persuasive in the best way."

He rubs the tip of the pool stick thoughtfully, a sinister smile creeping onto his face.

"I can show you better than I can tell you." he declares, shifting his gaze to Mr. Grande, watches intently, ready for whatever comes next.

"Let me persuade you." Deamonotay continues, his voice dripping with confidence as he walks behind Mr. Torres, the pool stick firmly in his grasp.

Mr. Torres' voice echoing in the cold, dimly lit room. Laced with panic, and anger, "When I get out of this, I swear you have no idea who you're messing with!" "Do you hear me? Hey, hey, let me out of this! What are you motherfucking doing? What are you doing? You can't do this! I'm not signing the papers! I'm not signing the papers! Do you hear me!"

His desperate words fell into silence, met only by the oppressive atmosphere and the looming figure of Deamonotay, who stood poised to make his point clear. Mr. Torres strained against the restraints, trying to glimpse what Deamonotay was doing behind him. The oppressive silence thickened. Exhaustion seeped into Mr. Torres. His initial fervor dimming under the weight of futile struggle, "Come on man! Stop this! Stop this!" he pleaded. Desperation creeping into his tone. A defeated presence settled over him, the reality of his situation sinking in.

He fell into silence, mirroring the stillness of the three other men in the room.

Then a loud noise erupted from Deamonotay, slicing through the tension like a knife "Aaahhhh!!". The sound reverberated through the cold room, causing Mr. Torres's eyes to widen and his body to tense involuntarily. A loud *ding* echoed from the metal slab to which he was strapped, sending a jolt of fear through him. He clenched his eyes tightly, muscles rigid, for ten long seconds. Suddenly, he realized nothing had happened to him. Cautiously, he opened one eye, scanning the room in bewilderment.

To his surprise, all Deamonotay had done was strike the metal slab between Mr. Torres's legs with a hammer.

Deamonotay erupted into laughter as Mr. Torres's body shook uncontrollably, caught in the throes of shock. With a smirk on his face, he turned to Mr. Grande, who observed the spectacle with a serious demeanor.

"No! Mr. Torres, what do you think we are? We don't want you to leave here with the wrong impression. Absolutely not!", Deamonotay continued. "Now, I made a pilgrimage to the Holy Land. You can read about it, but it's not until you actually see the historical locations and artifacts that it becomes more real than ever. Do you know what amazed me the most, huh?"

Mr. Torres remained silent, staring at Deamonotay, uncertain of how to respond.

At that moment, Mr. Grande rolled a metal cart beside him, atop which rested a long, ominous box. Deamonotay approached the cart, opening the latches with deliberate slowness before lifting the lid.

"What impressed me the most was a thing called the '*Cat of Nine Tails*'," Deamonotay declared, slowly pulling the instrument from the box.

The moment Mr. Torres saw it, his eyes widened in horror.

"Some believe its name was given because of the nine straps or the cat-like scars it would inflict on human skin," Deamonotay explained, holding the whip with a mix of reverence and pride. "But the Romans, being supreme in torture, took it up a notch and added different pieces of sharp objects so that when it came across the body, it tore away flesh—irreparable damage. Like today, modifying an illegal AR."

Deamonotay gazed at the whip in amazement.

"I had to have an authentic one," he said. "I paid a lot to get it through customs—for moments like these."

Mr. Grande shoved the large hog hanging on a hook toward the metal slab where Mr. Torres was strapped. Then, with a deliberate motion, Mr. Grande approached and took the whip from Deamonotay.

"I believe before we go to a place of no return, a demonstration should be given," Mr. Grande said.

He dangled the straps of the whip in front of Mr. Torres, the metal tips glinting ominously.

Mr. Torres's eyes widened, panic setting in as he stared at the looming threat.

With a loud grunt, Mr. Grande swung the whip toward the hog. The sound of its movement cut sharply through the air. Mr. Torres closed his eyes in discomfort as blood splattered profusely all over Mr. Torres' face and body.

Mr. Grande finished and turned his gaze toward Mr. Torres.

Deamonotay stepped over to the hog, leaning in to examine the ripped-open back.

"Beautiful job, Grande. Precision cuts." Deamonotay said, admiring the carnage.

Walking over to Mr. Torres, he placed a hand on his back, the touch cold and deliberate.

"Mr. Torres, is there anything you want to say before we begin?" he asked, his voice calm yet menacing.

"I'll sign the fucking contract!" Mr. Torres shouted, his voice trembling with desperation. "Give me a pen! I'll sign the fucking contract!"

Deamonotay's lips curled into a smug smile.

"Yes, I believe we could have come to a reasonable resolution." he said, motioning to the others. "Clean him up and bring me his signature."

Without another word, Deamonotay and Mr. Grande left the room, their footsteps fading as the air grew still.

Deamonotay, Mr. Grande, and the driver sat in the SUV, now dressed in their original clothes. The windows were rolled down to let in the evening air. The sound of footsteps grew closer as Daniel approached, a folder in his hand. He flipped it open, holding it up for Deamonotay to see. Inside, the contract bore Mr. Torres's signature.

"He couldn't sign fast enough." Daniel remarked, a hint of amusement in his voice.

"Wonderful." Deamonotay said with a satisfied smile. "The easy work has been done. Now the hard work begins. I'll see you at the meeting tomorrow."

Daniel nodded. "Okay, I'll be there."

Deamonotay glanced at him pointedly.

"Formal." Deamonotay reminded.

Daniel shrugged nonchalantly. "Okay."

With that, the SUV pulled away, the rumble of the engine fading into the distance as Daniel watched them leave.

Chapter 7
The Negotiations

As the new day dawns, D.J. waits at the entrance of the designated site, flanked by a pair of bodyguards, watching Tomas and Hector emerge from a SUV, straightening their freshly new suits.

"Hey, Hector. Now, Tomas, let me congratulate you on handling that problem at my niece's school. Dear to my heart." he says with a nod. "And congrats on what I promised you—a partnership in what I have Tomas."

"Being here is me introducing you to the negotiation side of the business. Come on."

Security flanks D.J., guiding him, Tomas, and Hector toward the meeting location. His pace is brisk, his demeanor sharp as he speaks.

"I meet with certain people we do business with to make sure everything's running smoothly. Sometimes it's new business, updates, negotiations. I like it to be short and sweet so I can get the fuck out of here."

He glances back at Tomas, a wry grin on his face.

"Now remember, none of these people know who you are. All they need to know is you've come on board to my team as a minority partner, and you two are here, hands-on."

Before stepping forward, D.J. pauses to adjust his tie, casting a look back at both of them.

"These guys are ravage animals. The stories I've heard...never forget that."

Tomas and Hector exchange a glance, absorbing his words.

"That's the reason for the suits," D.J. continues, a hint of amusement crossing his face. "It's been proven that behaviors are usually tapered when dressed good. So we all agree to wear suits when we meet—a sign we'll be professional in this jungle. Nonetheless, a snake is a snake, no matter how you dress it. Take my lead."

Security remains stationed in front of the hangar, ensuring a perimeter of safety. Only one guard accompanies D.J., Tomas, and Hector as they step inside the spacious area where the meeting is set to unfold.

A long table dominates the space, surrounded by chairs, creating a stark contrast to the tension that fills the air. Deamonotay, Daniel, and Mr. Grande are already present, along with another security guard. Deamonotay is seated, his demeanor relaxed, while his brother pours himself a drink, waiting for the newcomers. Mr. Grande stands at attention, his posture exuding readiness.

"And they say we're the ones late. Let the truth be told," Daniel quips, taking a hearty gulp from his glass.

D.J. strides confidently toward the long table, his presence commanding attention.

"Pardon our tardiness. My two minority partners found it hard to find this place," D.J. says, introducing Tomas and Hector.

Tomas and Hector nod respectfully, standing alongside the security guard as D.J. takes his seat at the table.

"Tomas and Hector," Deamonotay begins with a sardonic smile. "Next meeting, you're bringing abuela and the quinceanera party. Is that what we're doing?"

"These gentlemen are essential to the infrastructure of my business." D.J. interjects smoothly. "I brought them here to be my advisors at this level, that's all."

"I hope that it is truly all." Deamonotay replies, his eyes narrowing slightly. "I like to know the people I get in bed with."

"You are in good hands," D.J. assures him, his tone confident. "Shipments are always on time. The chemist is the best in the country, producing the most potent pills. They're getting the most bang for their buck. That's why they look specifically for our product. Like top cold medicine. "

"There's a bad cold in the street," Daniel adds, a smirk on his lips.

"Yes." Deamonotay agrees, leaning forward. "And we're going to need more than just medicine."

D.J.'s interest piques.

"You need more? What are we talking about?"

"Real estate." Deamonotay states firmly. "We know your corporation has monopolized ownership of substantial property in Little Haiti. It allows you to build and do your illegals on your own property. See, 70% of Miami is Spanish and owned by the Spanish, but by default, you also have ownership of real estate where non-Spanish people have lived for decades—particularly Little Haiti."

"We own that land outright," D.J. asserts, his voice steady.

"You own that land like King said in the sixties. It was given to you." Deamonotay retorts, his intensity rising. "You know we're not invited to eat at the table."

D.J. replied. His expression unyielded. "You're eating like a king, Deamonotay."

"We're eating good, but we're not eating right." Deamonotay insists, his frustration palpable. "White people own white land. Red people own red land. Spanish people own Spanish land. Black people should own black land."

"I don't have a problem with that." D.J. responds, maintaining his composure. "But that's my property, from which I make a great profit, and I already have plans for development." "Plans for gentrification!" Deamonotay's warns, shaking his head. "We know how it's run, and we can't let that happen!"

The air between them feels thick as D.J.'s face hardens.

"Let that happen? What are you thinking you're talking about—"

Deamonotay's face remains impassive, his gaze steady. "We're talking about inviting us to the table by doing what your people did before you. Give us the land." "We're not saying for free. We're willing to pay a pleasing price for you to release what's rightfully ours to control. It's our time to eat at the table. Or do you think of us like animals, only fed the scraps?"

The silence stretches long and tense as D.J. takes in the words. Tomas and Hector exchange a glance, sensing the atmosphere shift.

A flicker of tension passes between Deamonotay and Daniel. Mr. Grande's fists clench, his massive frame shifting forward—a silent threat.

"Mr. Grande," Deamonotay raises a hand, signaling for restraint.

Grande halts, though his eyes stay fixed on D.J., smoldering with restrained anger.

D.J.'s expression remains unreadable as he finally answers.

"Of course not. You know I respect you all. I paused because you present a proposition that requires not a quick answer—it will require more time."

Deamonotay lets his hand fall, nodding slightly.

"Please forgive Mr. Grande. You know, in French it's 'Grand.' In English, it's 'Mr. Big.' But in Spanish, 'Grande' just rolls off the tongue better. He's my strong arm when the time is right." his gaze sharpening. "But D.J., time is exactly what we don't have. Get back with us quickly on what you've decided."

He rises from the table, giving a single nod.

"Gentlemen."

Deamonotay, Daniel, and Mr. Grande leave the room, their footsteps echoing as they go. The tension follows them into the hallway.

Daniel's voice breaks the silence as they walk. "He's not going to give us the property,"

"You get everyone's attention when the noose tightens," Deamonotay replies coldly. "So let's start tightening the noose."

Back in the meeting room, Tomas, Hector, and D.J. remain, the weight of the encounter settling around them.

Tomas speaks first, breaking the silence.

"You know they're changing the dynamics of the deal. It might be more than you want to give."

"There's always someone trying to switch lanes midstream. Nevertheless, you've got to be ready when they're trying to change you."

D.J. eyes are hard and steady. "I'm ready for whatever they bring us. And since we have these suits on, we are definitely ready for the next engagement."

Tomas raises a brow, a faint smirk forming.

"You want us to go somewhere?"

"Yeah, but this is fun and classy. You've got to know how to pivot."

Hector chuckles. "We can't waste a good opportunity with a good suit."

D.J.'s eyes gleam with a hint of mischief.

"Believe me, where I'm taking you, you'll stand out."

Chapter 8

School Recital

On the stage of a school auditorium, a young boy performs for a school recital. In the audience, D.J., Tomas, and Hector sit among the parents. Tomas and Hector glance around, looking confused about being in this type of setting. As the young boy finishes, applause fills the room.

The MC steps up to the mic. "Great job, Nicholas! Now, we'll have a beautiful piano recital by Tiffany Santana."

The audience claps in anticipation as Tiffany walks up to the piano and begins to play, filling the room with a breathtaking melody. Tomas, entranced, watches in amazement as the young girl delivers a flawless performance. When she finishes, the applause is louder than before, with D.J., Tomas, and Hector joining in enthusiastically.

With the recital over, D.J., Tomas, and Hector linger in the school foyer. Tomas looks around, observing how the other parents are dressed.

"I feel so overdressed," Tomas says, shifting uncomfortably.

D.J. grins. "You look like money. That's the way you're supposed to look hanging with me. It's always better to be overdressed than under."

Hector nods toward the crowd. "You don't see how these single mothers are looking at us? I don't know about you, but I'm dressed just right."

At that moment, Tiffany rushes up to D.J.

"Uncle D.J.!" she exclaims, embracing him.

"Dolce Maraposa!" D.J. replies, holding her tight. "You did a splendid job. I am so proud of you."

Tiffany pulls back, smiling nervously. "I was so nervous."

"No, you were so prepared. I told you—what you practice is what you perform, and you performed magnificently."

He turns to introduce her. "Gentlemen, this is my niece, Tiffany."

Hector nods approvingly. "You did a great job, little lady."

Tomas steps forward, reaching out his hand. "Let me be the first to shake the hand of the one I see playing in Carnegie Hall. her own concert—I called it first."

He shakes her hand with a smile.

From a distance, Tiffany's mother, Rosa, notices Tomas shaking her daughter's hand. She excuses herself from a conversation with other parents and heads toward them.

"What is Carnegie Hall?" Tiffany asks curiously.

D.J. chuckles. "It's a great concert venue where all the greats perform. I talk like I've been there, but that's what I've heard—and I see you there someday."

"Oh, thanks." Tiffany says, beaming.

Rosa reaches the group and smiles warmly. "So, Uncle, you made it."

She hugs D.J., giving him a kiss on the cheek.

"You act like you're surprised. I couldn't miss your daughter's recital. Magnifica! Magnifica!" he exclaims, beaming with pride. "Yes, you were so wonderful. I told you, you were going to get through it with a breeze. A professional!"

Rosa praises. Smiling at her daughter..

"A Carnegie Hall professional. That's what I told her." Tomas adds with a grin.

Turning to Rosa, he introduces his companions. "Rosa, this is Tomas and Hector. We're going to do some major business together."

Rosa greets them warmly. "Hey, nice meeting you all. Carnegie Hall, huh?" She glances at Tiffany. "You know what's synonymous with Carnegie Hall?"

One of D.J.'s security team steps up, whispers something, and hands him a cell phone.

Tiffany shakes her head. "No. What?"

In unison, Rosa and Tomas reply, "Practice."

They exchange a knowing look, both amused.

"Oh, you heard that too?" Tomas chuckles.

"Excuse me, y'all, as I take this call," he says, stepping away.

Watching him leave, Rosa gestures toward the refreshment table. "Why don't you guys get some refreshments before they run out? Tiff, take them over there."

"Okay," Tiffany agrees, leading the way.

As they start to follow, Rosa stops Tomas. "Let me talk to Mr. Tomas for a moment. He'll catch up with you in a minute." she says to Tiffany and Hector.

After they walk off, Tomas watches Tiffany with a smile. "She's a sweet individual..."

Rosa turns to Tomas. Her sweet face has suddenly metamorphose and hardens.

"Get your motherfucking ass away from my daughter! Do you hear me! If I see you around her again, I'll kill you. Do you hear me! Huh?"

Tomas takes a step back, stunned. "Hey, what is this? Jekyll and Hyde? Whoa. All I was doing was giving a compliment!"

"She doesn't need to hear that from people like you." Rosa snaps.

"People like me! Hold up. What kind of person do you think I am?"

"I know the people my uncle does business with. I work with my uncle. I see what my uncle does, and I don't want that around my daughter. Do you hear me?"

"Hey, what kind of person do you think I am? You don't know me!" Tomas retorts, his face reddening.

Rosa glares at him, her voice ice cold. "I know all I need to know. Stay the fuck away from her!"

With that, Rosa turns on her heel and strides away, leaving Tomas standing there, anger boiling beneath the surface.

Chapter 9
She Did What??

I nside the SUV, the atmosphere is filled with laughter. D.J., Tomas, and the security team cruise down the road, but Tomas seems less than thrilled as D.J. and Hector laugh at his expense.

"She did what?" Hector manages between laughs, clearly entertained.

Tomas just shakes his head, sighing.

"That sounds like my niece." D.J. says, grinning. "She can be a firecracker. You got the good side."

"The good side!" Tomas echoes, incredulous.

Hector laughs even harder, the amusement on his face only growing.

"Yeah," D.J. continues, leaning back comfortably. "That's why she's one of my top lieutenants. Don't let the PTA dress fool you. She's head of my security."

"She was strapped," he adds. "You better be happy she didn't pull out on you."

"Head of your security?" Hector asks, surprised.

Tomas nods, thinking back on his encounter with her. "Nah, I can believe it. The way she looked at me."

"No doubt." D.J. flashes a sarcastic smile. "She was given a name—Black Widow," D.J. clarifies.

"Black Widow?" Tomas exclaims, surprised. "That's not a name you get at a sewing club."

"Definitely not," Hector agrees. "Your whole strategy was off. You were messing with what she's most sensitive about—her daughter," he adds. "With women like that, you've got to go in direct."

D.J. chuckles, his eyes twinkling with amusement, while Hector doubles over in laughter once more. Once the laughter dies down, D.J. leans forward.

"Well, I got a call. We got our shipments coming in this Tuesday. I'll take you by then so you can see how the operation works."

Chapter 10

Toss & Turn

It's a rainy Miami night, and the storm's distant rumbling seeps into the room. Tomas lies tangled in his bed, the top cover thrown off, dressed only in his boxers. His skin glistens with sweat as he tosses and turns, caught in a nightmare.

In the dream, he's 17 again, standing in front of his mother, his voice straining as he pushes for answers he's wanted his whole life.

"Can you at least tell me where he's buried?" he asks, his tone sharp with frustration.

"Buried? Why is that so important? Where he's buried? Your father is dead." she snaps back.

"Because he's my father! Why is it such a big deal? What happened? Why is it such a secret? Can you give me that?" His words spill out in a mixture of anger and desperation.

Her face hardens, but she doesn't look away.

"It's not a secret. It's a dark cloud that's trying to cast over this family, and I've managed to keep it away."

Tomas shakes his head, incredulous.

"What are you talking about, Mom? You've done your job, and you've done a good job. I'm telling you—I still feel incomplete not knowing about my other side."

A tremor of emotion crosses her face, and she finally releases the truth.

"Your father was a killer. A prominent drug dealer."

Stunned, Tomas stares at her, his mind reeling.

"He worked with some dangerous people," she continues. "People who were jealous of his rise and later turned on him. He decided to turn state's evidence, and we went into the witness protection program. Somehow, they found where we were and killed him. I was able to get away, and then I found out I was pregnant with you."

She pauses, her eyes full of sorrow and fear.

"I feared they might soon find me, so I left the witness protection program, got off the grid, and went into hiding."

Tomas is speechless, the weight of her words pressing down on him.

"What else do you want to know?" she asks, a resigned sadness in her voice. "I'll tell you whatever you want to know. You just have to promise me one thing—that whatever I tell you, you won't be like him. That's all I ask."

"Of course not. I promise." he says, his voice barely a whisper, repeating the words as though trying to make them real. "I promise. I promise."

The scene fades as Tomas jolts awake, his heart pounding. The room is dark, but the storm outside crashes on—the rain pelting against the window and thunder rumbling in the distance. Tomas swings his legs over the edge of the bed, sitting there in the dark, still shaken.

Chapter 11
Distribution

At the Miami port, a dock worker directs a trailer loaded with boxes of pills toward a waiting semi-truck. He hands the semi driver a clipboard to sign, and beneath it, a discreet envelope of cash slides into the dock worker's hand. The driver climbs into the cab and pulls out of the port, passing an old car where three figures—D.J., Tomas, and Hector—watch silently.

A semi packed with boxes of pills sits parked beside a building across the street. A figure steps out of a car and retrieves a key hidden in a nearby trash can. Unlocking the semi, the figure climbs in and drives off. One of D.J.'s guys, disguised as a homeless man leaning on a gate, watches the whole scene unfold. Then, he gets up, walks over to the abandoned car, opens the trunk, and finds a suitcase full of cash. Checking under the mat for the key, he closes the trunk, gets into the car, and drives away.

D.J., Tomas, and Hector observe every movement from a distance.

Later, they're at the Fort Lauderdale airport, standing near a terminal with large windows. Hector points out an import plane on the tarmac. A work van is parked by it, and four men are loading several cases of pills into the back. D.J. gives Tomas a knowing look, and Tomas nods, taking it all in.

Inside a warehouse, a large metal table is covered with pills. Several women, barely clothed, work around the table, packing the pills into small plastic bags while guards patrol nearby. D.J. leads Tomas and Hector into the room, gesturing to the operation.

In a sprawling hangar, men transport boxes of pills from one van to another. Rosa, armed and vigilant, directs the security team. D.J., Tomas, and Hector join Rosa in the hangar. They wait on Deamonotay.

Tomas slides over to Rosa, introducing himself casually.

"Hi, Ms. Widow."

"Excuse me?" Rosa responds, clearly confused.

"Black Widow. Isn't that what they call you?" Tomas probes.

Rosa shoots him a sharp look from the corner of her eye.

"What has that to do with anything?" she retorts, her tone clipped.

"I mean, to get that name, you must have done some serious things." Tomas presses, intrigued.

Rosa replies firmly, "If you keep asking questions, I can arrange for you to find out."

"Whoa, what a crass tongue. Does it shoot a web too?" Tomas quips sarcastically.

"No, but it'll do a good job cursing you out. Now get away from me." she snaps, her adamant tone leaving no room for debate.

Suddenly, Deamonotay, Daniel, and Mr. Grande emerge from an office, flanked by their own security. The guards are dragging a young man, bound and struggling, toward two semi-trucks parked outside.

"D.J., I'm so glad you made it to this delivery." Deamonotay says, his voice pleasant but firm. "But I must admit. I'm disappointed that you haven't responded to my proposal."

D.J. nods, calm but unwavering.

"Deamonotay, I hope my presence here reassures you that I'm not avoiding you. At this time, I don't see how it can happen. I hope you understand that."

Deamonotay's eyes narrow. "I understand that you might be underestimating the seriousness of this matter."

His security team begins chaining the young man between the two semi-trucks as he struggles against the bonds, his muffled screams barely audible through the tape over his mouth. Deamonotay strolls over to a table where two open suitcases filled with cash sit. One of D.J.'s men inspects the stacks of money.

D.J. sits across the table, with Tomas and Hector standing beside him.

"My people are being mishandled." Deamonotay continues, "We need our own infrastructure, built by our own hands. We'll do business with you, but not as renters or guests on our own land. We offered a fair proposition for all the properties."

Hector mutters, "What does this guy think he is, Robin Hood?"

"Yeah, I'm Robin Hood, you dumb fuck!" Deamonotay snaps back. "But I'm not using no fucking bow and arrows. We're all allergic to lead, motherfucker!"

Hector retorts, "Yeah? Well, I bet you're about to find out how allergic you can be."

Tomas puts a firm hand on Hector's shoulder.

"Hector!" D.J.'s voice cuts through the tension.

The room falls silent. D.J. tries to bring down the hostile temperature, "Let's remain professional, gentlemen."

Deamonotay hears the young man's muffled cry and takes his seat.

"Yes! We are gentlemen." Deamonotay says slowly, his voice low. "With the propensity to be savages. For example, the man behind me was a top-level guy in my organization. Someone I elevated."

He raises one hand, and the two semi-trucks begin to pull in opposite directions. The young man's chains go taut, lifting him slightly off the ground. D.J., Tomas, and Hector watch, their expressions unreadable, though their eyes remain fixed on the scene, unable to look away.

"Some would say, 'My man, one hundred grand." Deamonotay says, his voice growing louder as he gestures with his hands, "but he took my meekness for weakness. He tested our relationship."

He raises both hands, pushing them farther apart, and the trucks inch further away. The young man's body contorts, his joints straining, his screams choked by the tape. His hands and ankles dislocate, his spine bending unnaturally until only his head and limbs are visible from behind.

"And you know what happens when you don't make it right?" Deamonotay growls. "When you don't make amends? When you don't settle your trespasses?"

He thrusts his arms wide open, and the trucks pull even further apart until the young man's body—splits in half behind him. A visceral splatter of blood coats the ground streaming down a nearby drain.

Deamonotay stands in front of the gruesome display, unfazed.

"I know it tears him up that we won't be doing business together." he says, his gaze lingering on each face. Then, rising from his chair, he adds, "Let's finalize this matter in the next few days....gentlemen." His tone is cool and measured.

With that, he strides away, Mr. Grande and Daniel following close behind.

D.J., Tomas, and Hector remain rooted to the spot, standing in silence as they process what they've just witnessed.

Deamonotay walks away, with Mr. Grande and Daniel trailing behind him.

D.J., Tomas, and Hector remain standing, still reeling from the brutal display.

Tomas breaks the silence, his voice low.

"What did this psycho son of a bitch just show us?"

D.J. answers, a grim finality in his tone.

"War."

Chapter 12

Secret Escape

In D.J.'s office at the mansion, Tomas and Hector are present. D.J. sits at his desk while Hector occupies a chair, and Tomas stands, tension radiating from him.

"Let me take a team of your men. Let me go down there and handle business before they get us. I'll be damned if they tie us up and start playing Mr. Elastic Man!" Hector urges.

D.J. replies calmly, "What Deamonotay was doing is trying to force a seat at the table. We are different. If you have to use that, it's for protection. A strong defense is a strong offense."

Hector retorts, his frustration evident, "We should hit them first to let them know we mean business—to back the fuck up!"

Tomas asks with curiosity, "D.J., why won't you sell them the land?"

D.J. raises an eyebrow at the implication. "The lands are already tied up in contract deals with big-time developers. Deals that have been in play going on two—some three—years. For me to switch lanes and do what Deamonotay is asking can't happen. In a sense, he's right. They weren't invited to be part of the table, and when people aren't invited, I shouldn't be surprised when they crash the party."

Tomas questions, "If war is enivitible, then..." Just then, Rosa enters the office, looking good in a tight-fitted outfit that accentuates her figure."

"Okay, Uncle, what is the plan for those lunatics?" she asks, her tone a mix of curiosity and concern.

As she passes, Tomas notices how fine she looks but tries not to be too obvious.

D.J. looks up. "Why are you so dressed up?"

Rosa reaches into her purse and pulls out her earrings, starting to put them on. "I have to meet with a realtor in an hour. And remember, this coming Thursday, I have a swim teacher coming to use your pool for Tiffany's swimming lessons."

"Oh, that's right. Tomas and Hector just found a place. You might be able to use their realtor." D.J. replies.

Rosa turns to Tomas but noticed that Tomas was checking her out. He quickly turns his head.. Her expression shifts from bewilderment to disgust.

"Nah, I'm good. And don't have your little hoochies around the pool either. Remember Tiffany," she snaps.

D.J. raises an eyebrow. "What are you talking about? She can come over anytime. Plus, I need you to have a two-man rotating detail watching Deamonotay's moves. We need to be informed when they're making a move."

"I'm on it. I'll have a detail on them starting tonight. I want to fuck them up anyway after what I saw them do to that guy." Rosa growls.

D.J. notices Tomas is trying hard not to look in Rosa's direction.

"Tomas, you were saying something?" D.J. prods.

"What? I'm good." Tomas replies.

"Are you sure? I mean, I think since Rosa is here, she might want to hear any concerns you might have."

Rosa turns her head and looks at Tomas. He notices her gaze on him.

"You said it was war. If war comes to your front door, are you fully prepared? I see the security all around. Is it enough?" Tomas challenges.

D.J. smirks, and Rosa looks amused.

"The guys you see are only part of the team. There's a team you don't see. There are guns all around this mansion—not one room where you're not protected. If they make it to this room, we have some crazy tricks in store for them. This is like the Enterprise. We can control everything from here."

Rosa picks up a large remote control system and starts pressing buttons. The security screens light up, displaying the floor plan of the house with live visuals.

D.J. rises from his chair and walks to the bookshelf behind him. Rosa pushes another button on the controller, and a metal door opens behind the bookshelf.

Tomas and Hector move closer to the secret entrance.

"Look at this—some secret service shit." Hector says, wide-eyed.

"Wow!" Tomas breathes.

D.J., Tomas, and Hector peer inside to find a fireman's pole.

"The wall behind this bookshelf is three feet thick. This door is reinforced steel—a tank would have a problem coming through here," D.J. explains. "I come in here with the remote, hit the lock button—no one comes in or out. This pole leads down to an underground garage to a custom bulletproof BMW. It goes straight through a tunnel to the private golf course next door. I drive across the green, hit the freeway—perfect getaway."

Tomas shakes his head in disbelief.

"This is what you call a rabbit hole for the rich." Rosa says.

"Got to go, fellas. I'll talk to you later, uncle."

Placing the controller on D.J.'s desk, she walks out.

Tomas watches her leave, and D.J. leans over to him.

"If you stare at the flame too long, you'll go blind."

Chapter 13
Construction Site Set-Up

In Little Haiti, construction is underway on one of D.J.'s properties. A work van pulls onto the site unnoticed by the crew. Four Haitian men emerge from the van, wearing construction hats and vests. Two of the men keep watch outside, while the other two enter the trailer where the construction head is busy on the phone.

The construction head speaks into the phone. "Yeah, I need that cement by tomorrow so we can start pouring." He pauses, then asks, "Hold on. Can I help you?"

The two men who entered open their toolboxes and pull out guns with silencers. They signal for the construction head to hang up.

"Let me call you back. I have to tend to an emergency." he stammers nervously, hanging up the phone.

Meanwhile, D.J. is driving in his Mercedes when his car phone rings. He answers.

"Angel, what's happening?"

"We have a problem,\." the construction head replies urgently. "Vandals have come, broken the glass we need to install, stolen the lumber and supplies. The police are here and need you to come by to answer some questions for the police report."

D.J. mutters, "These little maricones... You can't put the police on the phone?"

The construction head pauses. "No. He needs to see you in person."

D.J. feels his frustration mounting. "Okay, I'm ten minutes away."

He hangs up and immediately calls Tomas and Hector.

Tomas picks up. "Yo?"

"I just got vandalized at one of the properties. I'll text you the address. Meet me there."

"We're on the way." Tomas replies, and D.J. hangs up.

D.J. pulls up to the property, parks, and gets out of the car. He reaches behind him, pulls out his gun, and tucks it securely under the driver's seat.

Before starting toward the trailer, his eyes scan the area, looking for signs of vandalism, but nothing immediately stands out. He spots a construction worker nearby.

"Where's Angel?" D.J. asks.

The construction worker nods toward the trailer. "I think he's in there."

"And the police?" D.J. inquires, eyebrows raised.

The worker frowns, looking puzzled. "Police? I don't know anything about police."

D.J. keeps walking, still scanning the area. Behind two of the porta-potties, two of the Haitian men hold assault weapons, waiting for the right moment. A construction worker drives a dump truck slowly past the porta-potties, giving the men cover as they move closer to D.J., hiding behind the truck.

As D.J. approaches the trailer, D.J.'s gaze sweeps the area, still looking for a police car as he edges closer. Suddenly, the dump truck shifts, revealing the two men with their weapons drawn.

Realizing it's a setup, D.J. bolts for cover behind some construction supplies. The two men in the trailer emerge, guns blazing, aiming their fire at D.J. The construction site erupts in chaos as workers scramble to escape the crossfire.

D.J. starts running, dodging between construction materials as bullets fly. Panicked construction workers scatter—scrambling to escape. He ducks behind a stack of beams, catching his breath just long enough to see the four Haitian men closing in, guns ready.

He takes off again, scaling several stories up the skeletal structure. Finally, he reaches a narrow metal beam high above, shimmying onto it cautiously, finding a small pocket of cover. D.J. realizes he has nowhere to go—trapped high above the ground. He glances over the edge of the skyscraper, calculating if jumping would be a better fate than being riddled with bullets.

The wind whips around him as he contemplates his last desperate move. The four Haitian men inch closer, guns pointed straight at D.J. as they edge along separate beams, sealing off every possible escape. D.J. steadies himself, eyes darting, searching for an opening—yet there's none in sight. With clenched fists, D.J. prepares for his fate.

Suddenly, the air explodes with the sharp crack of gunfire. One by one, the men are struck. Caught off guard, they lose balance and fall from the beams, plunging to their deaths below.

D.J. glances down to see Tomas and Hector standing below, assault weapons still raised—his redemptors.

Chapter 14
Then War It Is

A s the cars rolled to a stop on the gravel road, a couple of miles away from the construction site in danger, the secluded spot felt cloaked in a tense silence. Doors swung open in sync, and D.J., Tomas, and Hector stepped out. Their expressions hardened, each man fueled by the anger simmering in the air.

"In broad fucking daylight. They want to put a hit out on me in broad daylight," D.J.'s voice was a low, simmering rage, every word laced with venom.

"I'll get those bastards. It's war! They want war? It's war they'll get." Hector's voice was sharp, almost pleading. "I told you, let me take a team down there to clean house. They almost got the drop on us."

Tomas nodded, his frustration evident. "Almost. It was luck that we came when we did. They caught us with our pants down, unprepared because we're messing up, thinking like businessmen instead of strategic killers!"

He turned to D.J., his tone resolute. "No more Mr. Nice Guy. Heads got to roll."

D.J. clenched his fists, his voice low and determined. "Heads got to roll. You're right. And like you said, strategic first. We lock down our infrastructure. A move this bold to take me out? They must have thought they'd succeed."

He paused, his mind racing. "I need to head back to the construction site. Got to come up with an excuse because real police will be coming, and I'll need to reassure the investors that what happened today isn't connected to me."

Tomas' face was tense as he spoke, each word landing with weight. "You can't be roaming these streets alone. They came specifically for you. We'll be with you until Rosa can get you adequate security."

"Rosa!" D.J.'s gaze shifted as he thought aloud. "She's dropped Tiffany off for swimming lessons. You guys go down there and make sure the compound's locked down. And make sure to turn away the swim teacher. We can't have new faces popping up right now."

Tomas nodded, catching every instruction as D.J. continued. "Also, contact the pipeline to Little Haiti. We're drying them out from any product."

Hector nodded, staying close to D.J. Tomas turned to them both. "You stay with him, Hector." he said firmly, glancing at Hector. "I'll go to the mansion and make sure everything is straight. We'll keep updating each other by the hour."

D.J. replied, his tone steady but laced with tension. "If communication is broken, it means something has happened."

Without another word, Tomas got into his car while D.J. and Hector climbed into the other. Both vehicles pulled away, heading in different directions, each driver resolute in their mission.

Chapter 15
Tiffany's Tribulation

Tiffany lounged on one of the beach chairs, dressed in her bathing suit, waiting for the swim instructor. She pulled out her cell phone, slipping in her earbuds to tune out the world.

Tomas's car pulled up to the mansion with a sense of urgency. He stepped out, striding over to the two security guards stationed at the door, his voice calm but authoritative. "Did you tell the swim teacher his session was canceled?" he asked.

"Yeah," one of the guards replied. "He came, but we told him Rosa will call to reschedule."

Tomas nodded and stepped inside the mansion, one of the security guards following him in. "Did someone tell Tiffany he's not coming?" Tomas continued.

The guard hesitated. "No, we didn't know if we were the ones that could tell her."

"Cool." Tomas said, "Let Rosa do it."

At the pool Tiffany glanced at the time on her cell phone, her frustration mounting as she noticed the swim instructor was late. With a sigh, she walked over to the shallow end of the pool, sinking down onto the steps, letting the cool water calm her nerves.

Tomas turned toward the security guard, his voice steady but urgent. "Okay, make sure this place is locked down. I need to make some calls. When Rosa gets back, we'll meet with everyone to prepare for war. Miguel, no one new gets in."

The security guard replied, "Okay."

Tomas rushed up the stairs to D.J.'s office. He needed to handle things quickly as he made his way toward the room.

Meanwhile, Tiffany, eager to learn to swim, was determined to start practicing on her own. She spotted one of the arm flotation devices resting on the edge of the pool. Walking over to it, she slipped the flotation around one arm, then began searching for the other one. She noticed it floating on the deep side of the pool. Tiffany looked around, hoping to find something to pull it closer, but there was nothing within reach.

Inside the mansion, Tomas entered D.J.'s office. He walked up to D.J.'s desk and pressed a button. The panel in front of him shifted, revealing a hidden safe embedded into the base of a statue. He pulled out a record folder, placing it onto the desk before grabbing his phone to begin dialing. Tomas spoke into the phone, his voice low and controlled as he addressed the person on the other end.

"Michael! Yeah, it's me, Tomas. You heard what happened? Yes, everyone's fine. Listen, we're cutting off the valve to Little Haiti."

Meanwhile, Tiffany carefully slid down the deep side wall of the pool, determined to reach the arm float that had drifted further out of her reach. She tightly gripped the edge of the pool with one hand, stretching her other arm toward the flotation device. Her fingers brushed against it, but instead of grabbing hold, she accidentally pushed it further away from her. Now almost fully submerged, Tiffany extended herself as much as she could, only to lose her grip on the edge of the pool. She fluttered around, kicking up, only to find herself unwillingly submerging downward. Her eyes widened in alarm as the water rose around her.

Tomas spoke into the phone with urgency. "It's imperative that we disable Deamonotay and draw him out."

Tomas walked out onto the balcony, his eyes scanning the area below. As he looked beyond the railing, his gaze froze. There, at the bottom of the pool, was Tiffany's lifeless body. His heart skipped a beat. Tomas dropped the phone.

"Oh my God, Tiffany!"

In a split second, he bolted into action, rushing toward the balcony's railing. He climbs over it, then doesn't hesitate jumping into the pool. Tomas swam down, reaching Tiffany's motionless form. His heart pounded as he grabbed her, pulling her upward with adrenaline coursing through his veins. Tomas swam quickly to the edge of the pool, dragging her lifeless body out of the water. His hands shook as he tried to revive her, his voice thick with panic.

"Come on, baby, come on! What happened? You have to make it! Help!"

His voice was hoarse and desperate as he fought for her to breathe again. Tomas pressed his hands against Tiffany's chest, his movements precise but urgent as he began CPR. Still, there was no response. Desperation mounted in his voice.

"Come on! Help! Help somebody!"

He called out, his tone breaking. One of the security guards rushed into the pool area.

"Call 9-1-1!" Tomas barked without looking up, his focus entirely on Tiffany.

The guard quickly dialed, speaking urgently into the phone. Tomas leaned close, filled with an aching plea.

"Come on, angel, you've got to make it. Come on."

He continued the compressions, pressing down and releasing rhythmically, his determination unwavering.

"You are too young."

Suddenly, Tiffany's body jolted as she sputtered, coughing up water, her breaths ragged but returning. Tomas exhaled sharply in relief as a second security guard rushed over, then a third, alert and ready.

"There you go!" Tomas' face lighting up with relief. "Great job coming back. Great job!"

Finally, he sank to his hands and knees, overwhelmed and exhausted but relieved beyond words as he watched Tiffany breathe steadily once more.

As night progressed, Tomas sits on the back step of the emergency vehicle, draped in a blanket, his face a mix of exhaustion and relief. Hector and one of the security guards stood close by, keeping silent vigil. Across from them, Tiffany lay on a medical cot inside another emergency vehicle. D.J. hovered by her side watching, his face tense but steady.

The security guard turned to Tomas, his voice low but intense. "You're a damn guardian angel, you know that? If you hadn't been there, all hell would've broken loose. Even the devil himself wouldn't have shown his face if Rosa's daughter didn't make it."

Tomas looked over. He sees Rosa arriving, looking frantic as she rushes past everyone to get to Tiffany, wrapping her arms around her. Her face to Tiffany's ear whispering words of comfort.

Tomas sighed, the weight of the day settling heavily on him. "This is too much for one day, Hector. Just get me out of here."

"Let's go!" Hector said, helping him off the step of the vehicle.

Tomas rose slowly, glancing over at Rosa as she held Tiffany close, her hands brushing Tiffany's hair back gently. He let the blanket fall, taking a steadying breath as he and Hector headed toward the car.

Rosa turned her head to Tomas, realizing the hero is departing.

Chapter 16

Maybe it was, Maybe it wasn't

D.J. sat at his desk in his office, the glow of his computer screen casting a dim light across the room. Tomas and Hector were seated across from him, both men tense, their eyes focused on the Zoom call where Deamonotay's image flickered.

D.J. leaned forward, his fingers tapping against the surface of his desk, his voice cutting through the silence. "So let's do away with all the bullshit. So that was you at the construction site?" D.J. asked, his tone sharp.

Deamonotay's image on the screen showed a slight smirk, his response slow and calculated. "I was amazed at what happened at the construction site. When I heard, you are asking, was it me? Your main concern should be, are you doing the necessary things to right your wrongs? It seems danger is at your doorstep. Someone or somebody don't like your business. I heard you took care of many bodies this time. Maybe it's one, or a contract on everything."

The tension in the room thickened. Tomas stood, his voice low but simmering with anger. "You want to fuck with us? Do you really want to fuck with us? Do you think you can handle the shit storm we can rain on you?"

Deamonotay's image on the screen flickered as his voice grew louder, the tension palpable. "Who's talking? Tell them to come to the screen." he demanded. "D.J., are these your handlers?"

Tomas, his anger boiling over, stood up abruptly. He grabbed the laptop and turned it toward himself, his eyes never leaving the screen. "It's me, you son of a bitch. The only person who's about to get handled is you. When you threaten D.J., you threaten all of us. I don't think you understand who you're messing with."

Deamonotay's face twisted with disdain, his voice a sharp contrast. "Tomas, no, you don't!," he retorted. "I'm fighting for just 3.4 square miles. Yes, that's Little Haiti, but I have the resources of a country—the Republic of Haiti. So don't fuck with me and give me what I want!"

Behind Tomas, Hector stood, his own anger simmering, the muscles in his arms tensing as he stepped forward to respond. "You think you can hide behind all that power? You don't know who you're dealing with either." Hector stood, his posture tense as he pulled his gun from its holster and aimed it directly at the laptop screen, his eyes were locked on the image of Deamonotay.

D.J. glanced at Hector, then calmly reached over, turning the laptop to face himself. "I don't have to say anything." D.J. replies. "Not because they are my handlers. It's because they speak so eloquently on how I feel."

With a click, D.J. closed the laptop, effectively cutting off the connection with Deamonotay.

"He answered the question without answering." D.J. muttered to himself as he leaned back in his chair. "We have to beef up security on all construction projects. He understands that these 3.4 miles will generate billions. We can't have him causing havoc and fucking up the deal."

He looked up at Tomas and Hector, his voice now decisive. "I'll have Rosa get with you all to organize it. We have to look at where we can go on the offense with this guy instead of always being on the defense."

Chapter 17

Grande Gets Assassins

Deamonotay sat at his desk, his fingers tapping lightly on the closed laptop. As he pondered the conversation with D.J., his eyes fixed on the darkness across the room. In the silence, he called out, "Grande."

From the shadows, Mr. Grande stepped forward, his face partially illuminated by the dim light in the office.

"Get those Haitian assassins we used in D.C.," Deamonotay instructed, his voice calm but firm. "I have a couple of jobs for you."

Without a word, Mr. Grande nodded, then turned, disappearing into the hallway as he left to carry out the orders.

Chapter 18
Rosa says, 'Thank you!"

Tomas and Hector were at their shared house, where Hector was busy in the kitchen, stirring a pot on the stove with an air of satisfaction. Meanwhile, Tomas was settled on the couch, absorbed in a soccer game.

"See, we're living long because I put oregano in the sauce," Hector said, grinning as he gave the pot a good stir. "The special ingredient, vitamin K, the secret sauce."

Without taking his eyes off the TV, Tomas replied, "Oregano, vitamin K." He sighed. "You watch these cooking shows, and now everybody thinks they're a chef."

Hector looked at him, amused. "You know I put my foot in it."

Tomas replied, "Oh yeah, I can't deny it. It definitely tastes like there's a foot in it."

Hector couldn't believe what Tomas had said. "Then how come there's never no seconds? Tell me that."

Tomas didn't look up from the game. "I don't know. Maybe you got a friend..."

Just then, the doorbell rang. Tomas got off the couch, grabbed his gun out of habit, and walked to the door. He glanced through the window by the door, and his face registered surprise at the sight. He opened the door. Rosa stood there, her expression uncertain.

"Hi," she greeted him.

Tomas, clearly caught off guard, said, "Hey," glancing around as though trying to collect himself. "I wasn't expecting you here."

Rosa shifted slightly, looking around before speaking. "Um...Can I come in?"

"Oh yes. How rude." Tomas said, stepping aside. "Hector, look who's here."

Rosa walked inside, and Hector glanced up from his pot with a grin. "Hey, Rosa. Oh,uh...think I got enough? You staying for my surprise pasta?"

Tomas smirked and looked at Rosa. "I'll give away the surprise. He puts his foot in it."

Rosa looked between them, eyebrows raised. "Huh?"

"Don't listen to him," Hector replied, waving it off. "This is delicious."

Rosa offered a small smile. "I'm not going to stay long." She looked at Tomas, her expression tense. "I need to talk to you."

Tomas quickly glanced at the clutter on the couch and started shifting things aside. "Sure. Let me clean off the couch."

Rosa, with a commanding tone, said, "I'll meet you out in the back."

As she walked out, already heading toward the door that led to the backyard, Tomas turned to Hector with a small shrug. "Guess we'll meet in the back."

Tomas followed her. Outside he found Rosa pacing slightly, her gaze shifting as if lost in thought. He approached her, keeping his voice soft.

"Hey."

She stopped but kept moving her hands, a touch of nervous energy in her gestures.

Rosa brakes her silence. "I asked D.J. where you stayed. I wanted to tell you thank you for what you did."

Rosa took a deep breath, steadying herself. "I know I came at you hard. I'm a hard person. I've had a hard life. I apologize for how I treated you. I'm taking accountability for my actions of the past. I'm pushing down the wall I had between us."

Tomas exhaled, surprised. "I didn't see this coming."

She looked at him, her expression softening. "I'm hard, but you saved the softest part of me when you saved Tiffany."

Tomas replied, "I just did what needed to be done. Anybody would've done the same."

Rosa paused. "It wasn't just anyone—it was you. And I'm not about to let my past ruin something, like so many others do."

Tomas felt humbled and a tight knot in his chest. "Rosa, I don't think we're talking about the same thing. Plus, I'm not worthy... incredible woman, incredible daughter."

Rosa looked up at Tomas, her gaze steady and unwavering. "Your mouth may say no to me, but your eyes speak what you want. Tomas, look at me and tell me you don't want me."

She took a step closer, her face lifting toward his. Tomas averted his gaze, his eyes flicking upward as he tried to avoid her. His silence gave the answer, but his words confirmed it.

He murmured, "A hard woman giving a hard bargain."

Rosa's lips curved into a smile, a soft laugh escaping. "I'll have it no other way."

Tomas found himself smiling back and answered, "You hungry?"

"Let me take you out to eat. I don't think you want that foot in the pot."

Rosa's face shifted to surprise. "Does Hector really have a foot in the pot?"

"Bigfoot," Tomas replied.

The two shared a laugh as they stepped back into the house together.

Chapter 19

Grande Brings Assassins

Deamonotay and Daniel stood on the balcony, cigars in hand, smoke curling up into the night air. The mood was calm.

Mr. Grande entered the balcony with two figures at his side, hidden in shadow. Deamonotay's gaze fell on them.

"Good, good. You guys are here. Wonderful job you did in D.C. The police there are still baffled how it was done." he said, nodding approvingly. "Thank you for taking this job."

He paused, his eyes glinting as he took a drag from his cigar.

"Sometimes it's the wrong tactic attacking a man head-on. Sometimes the head is too strong. You have to attack his weakness—his foundation, his infrastructure. Then you'll see him buckle, and if you're lucky, see him crumble."

Daniel nodded.

Deamonotay continued, "When we get a lock on their location, I'll forward it."

He turned to Grande, his expression intensifying.

"Grande, I have a special task for you."

Chapter 20
Quality Time

As Tomas and Rosa spent days soaking in moments that felt stolen from a quieter, safer world, they cruised on a yacht, letting the breeze and the open water surround them. Dinner followed under soft golden lights, where conversation flowed as freely as the wine. They laughed together while driving, sharing quick kisses at red lights.

Later, they lay close in bed, tangled up in one another, savoring the warmth. In the kitchen, they moved around each other with ease, cooking side by side, stealing bites and small kisses between tasks. Their laughter filled the room.

One afternoon, Tomas sat at the piano, Tiffany beside him, practicing her scales as Rosa watched with a smile. It all felt almost unreal—simple, precious, and theirs.

Tomas and Rosa took care of their business affairs, cash stacked high in the safe at the house—excess wealth that seemed like more than they'd ever need. Together, they walked into a secret room with bills piled high, then down to the bank, depositing stacks of cash in five safety deposit boxes.

They dressed sharply, and Tomas slipped a sparkling necklace around Rosa's neck, his eyes admiring her elegance and strength from his spot on the balcony. D.J. would look out, watching as Tomas taught Tiffany to swim in the pool, patient and encouraging.

One morning, Tomas and Rosa dropped Tiffany off at school. She climbed out of the backseat, gave Rosa a quick kiss on the cheek, then turned to Tomas and, surprising him, wrapped her arms around his neck in a tight hug. Caught off guard by her affection, he then returned her hug warmly.

Tiffany waved, bounding off to school with a bright smile, and Rosa looked on, pleased and quietly content.

Chapter 21
Rosa Trying To Be Loving

The yacht cut smoothly across the water, a grand silhouette against the setting sun. Rosa stood at the front, her flowing outfit catching the breeze as she looked out at the endless expanse of the ocean. The yacht staff quietly worked nearby, tending to details until Tomas approached, something hidden behind his back.

Sensing his presence, the staff retreated indoors, leaving Tomas and Rosa to their own private moment. Tomas slipped an arm around her, and Rosa leaned back, a faint smile on her lips as she looked toward the horizon.

"It's hard for me to imagine this," she said softly.

"Imagine what?" he asked, his voice close.

"Sharing this moment." Rosa replied. "The sun, the water, this yacht—feeling special."

Rosa reached back, her fingers brushing his face. There was warmth in her eyes.

Tomas smiled. "Well, let's see if I get you with this." he said, pulling out a sleek gift box from behind his back.

Rosa turned around, her eyes lighting up with excitement. "I won't know how to act with all this jewelry you're giving me."

Silently, Tomas watched as she opened the box. Inside lay a beautifully crafted gun. Rosa's eyes widened in surprise and delight.

"You do get me!" she said, a hand over her mouth.

She turned and kissed him, the grin on her face radiating happiness. "I love it!"

Tomas chuckled. "It's the gift that keeps on giving. The bullets are in the cabin. You can try it out on the range when we go stateside tomorrow."

Rosa's expression turned playful. "Remember, we have to pick up Tiffany at my mom's tomorrow, so I'm going to shoot a couple of rounds before it gets dark."

Rosa broke away, excitement flashing in her eyes as she dashed toward the cabin.

"Where are the bullets?" she called back.

Tomas laughed, calling after her, "They're on the dresser in my closet."

He shook his head, a fond smile on his face as he watched her disappear into the cabin.

Chapter 22
The Tiffany Surprise

The car pulled up to Rosa's house. Tiffany, Rosa, and Tomas got out of the car. Tiffany rushed to the front door with just her handbag. Tomas headed to the back of the car to open the trunk and retrieve the luggage.

Rosa called out to Tiffany, "You better turn back around and get your bag. We're not going to be dealing with your stuff."

Tiffany stopped, turned back, and walked over to Tomas, who handed her the bag. She then opened the front door and rushed inside, quickly heading up the stairs toward her room.

"Don't throw that bag anywhere." Rosa reminded her. "Put it in your closet where it's supposed to be, young lady."

"Okay, Mom." Tiffany called back as she hurried up to her room.

Rosa dropped her bags in the Florida room and headed to the kitchen. Tomas entered the house with the luggage. Tiffany entered her room, threw her handbag on the bed, and then opened her closet door. She tossed her big bag inside, near her mountain of stuffed animals gathered in the corner. But Tiffany looked at the pile of stuffed animals again, her face filled with curiosity because the pile looked somewhat strange. All the eyes of the stuffed animals looked the same, but there were eyes looking directly at her.

All of a sudden, Mr. Grande sprang out from where her stuffed animals were and grabbed Tiffany.

In the kitchen, Rosa opened the refrigerator, grabbed a bottle of juice, and started drinking. Tomas placed the luggage by the stairs and heard a scream from upstairs. He heard it again and rushed upstairs, yelling, "Rosa!"

Rosa, confused, put the juice on the counter and hurried out of the kitchen. Tomas ran to Tiffany's room and pushed the slightly cracked door wide open. He saw Mr. Grande gagging Tiffany's mouth as she lay on the floor, tied with zip ties around her hands and feet. Mr. Grande saw Tomas and pulled out his Beretta from his back. Tomas charged Mr. Grande, and they both fell onto the bed and then onto the floor. The beretta slipped out of Mr. Grande's hand. Their fight spilled out of Tiffany's room into the hallway by the stairway.

Mr. Grande was dominating Tomas in the fight and saw Rosa trying to aim at him. He had pretty much subdued Tomas with punches and was holding Tomas's body between himself and Rosa.

Rosa realized she didn't have a clear shot at Mr. Grande from that range, so she started to run up the stairs. Mr. Grande saw Rosa coming closer, so he tossed Tomas's body down the stairs. Tomas's body hit Rosa, and they both fell to the ground floor. Tomas landed on top of Rosa, knocking the weapon out of her hand. It slid under the Florida room couch.

Mr. Grande began walking down the stairs. He stepped over Tomas and Rosa, moving them as he searched for the weapon Rosa had in her hand. All of a sudden, he remembered his gun was back upstairs. He turned around and started toward the stairs, with intent on retrieving his weapon.

Rosa, trying anything to stop Mr. Grande, resorted to kicking him with all her might between his legs. Mr. Grande cringed, recoiling in pain. As Rosa's kick landed, she got up and began to unleash a series of martial arts moves on Mr. Grande. Her strikes staggered him back, but he fought to regain his balance.

They struggled near a glass table and a cabinet, both of them pushing and pulling at each other in a chaotic battle for control. Rosa reached behind the cabinet, desperately trying to grab a hidden weapon, but her hand only brushed against it without success. Her fingers fell short of its grip.

Meanwhile, Tomas, barely conscious, stirred slightly. His body was heavy with exhaustion, and he struggled to push himself up, but he quickly slumped back down onto the floor. His eyes fluttered closed for a moment, but before they shut completely, he caught sight of Rosa's weapon lying just beneath the couch.

Rosa backed into the kitchen, her movements quick and defensive. As she continued to fight Mr. Grande, she darted toward the bottom drawer where the kitchen trash can was, hoping to find another hidden weapon. But before she could reach it, Mr. Grande intercepted her with a sudden attack. His strength overwhelmed her, and he gained the upper hand, leaving her body slumped in defeat.

Her head spun as Mr. Grande pulled her roughly by the collar, dragging her toward the sink. As they neared the counter, Rosa's eyes fell on the assortment of knives neatly arranged beside the sink. She realized his intentions—he was going for one of the knives. Just as his hand moved toward the blades, Rosa reacted quickly. With all the strength she had left, she grabbed his wrist, stopping him before he could make the grab.

A fierce struggle ensued as Rosa fought to resist him, her grip tightening around his hand in a desperate attempt to prevent him from seizing the weapon. Mr. Grande threw Rosa onto the kitchen counter, her body crashing near the assortment of knives. The sharp edges of the blades glinted in the light as she struggled to regain her footing, but the force of his attack left her momentarily dazed.

Rosa's eyes barely open sees the garbage disposal switch on the wall by her head. Desperation fueled her as she twisted her body, using all her strength to push his hands toward the sink. Mr. Grande stumbled forward under the force, and she managed to shove one of Mr. Grande's massive fingers into the sinkhole while holding down his wrist with all her might. She strained to reach the garbage disposal switch and turned it on.

Mr. Grande let out a horrible scream, his voice filled with agony and rage. He pulled his hand out of the hole to see it disfigured and bloodied. With his other hand, Mr. Grande punched Rosa. She becomes unconscious and slumps to the floor. Mr. Grande stumbled back and noticed the knives scattered across the floor. He bent over, picked up one of the blades, and raised it high above Rosa.

Suddenly, a gunshot rings out and a bullet burst through Mr. Grande forehead. More aggravated than dead, Mr. Grande takes his attention off Rosa and turns around to his assailant. Then quickly two shots hit his chest and another to the head drops the towering Mr. Grande dead. His bodily remains sprayed across the kitchen cabinets and on Rosa.

Tomas was standing there, holding Rosa's new weapon in his hand. He staggered to Rosa and slides down right next to her. Rosa, bruised and battered, remembered Tiffany was upstairs.

"Tiffany!" Rosa called.

Tomas helped Rosa up, and they tried to rush out of the kitchen.

Chapter 23

He Still Doing Business

In an office building conference room, the Brazilian investor sat at the polished conference table, his expression tense.

"This is something we can't take lightly," he exclaimed, his voice rising with urgency. "This is what all the local press is talking about. What did the detectives conclude about the incident at the construction site?"

Calm but firm, D.J. replied, "They assessed that rival gangs were trespassing, using the site as grounds to settle some beef. That's all."

Hector, stationed protectively by D.J., shifted his gaze toward the property investors.

The banker investor spoke up, his tone sharp. "Grounds to settle some beef? Didn't some people die at the site?"

D.J. met the question with a calm response. "When I got there, the detective said, unfortunately, four people are deceased."

The Spain investor leaned forward, his expression marked by concern. "This is why we're concerned, D.J. This isn't in any way connected to you?"

D.J. shook his head firmly. "No. This is about some punk kids using our property to settle a vendetta. That's all."

The room grew tense as the conversation shifted to the incident's repercussions.

"We can't be having negative press. That starts having people asking questions." one investor interjected, his tone edged with frustration. "People probing, then investigations halting our projected dates."

D.J. leaned back in his chair, exuding calm authority. "We're on schedule on all 12 properties. The Laguna Rising and the Multiplex Plaza are even ahead of schedule. I've added extra security at all the locations, making sure something like this doesn't happen again."

The Brazilian investor wasn't as easily placated. "But is that enough? Our associates have concerns, to see if we need to pull funding."

"Why would you pull out when we're so close?" D.J. countered, his voice steady and firm. "With anything of this magnitude, bumps in the road are to be expected."

"Yes," the Brazilian investor replied, narrowing his gaze, "but dead bodies are not to be expected. That's the kind of thing that puts a microscope on what we're doing."

The silence that followed was heavy, each man considering the stakes involved. D.J. remained calm, his voice steady as he addressed the concerns around the table.

"It would have if police suspected we had something to do with those deaths. But again, they assessed it as a random incident."

The Spain investor, still uneasy, leaned forward. "The picture we want to draw to the community is that we are upright businessmen, not thugs taking over a neighborhood block."

D.J. nodded, understanding the sentiment. "The bigger picture is the objective. Gentlemen, we're looking at $80 million in the first year. That's not a faucet I think your associates want to cut off so quickly."

The Spain investor seemed to weigh this, then spoke with more resolve. "With those numbers, we definitely won't. I think I can go back and give them reassurances that you have these developments under control."

The other investors paused in thought, considering the statement. The banking investor, still slightly cautious but with a shift in tone, spoke up.

"I think we can do the same."

The bank investor looked at the other investors with a nod, and they looked back at him, returning the gesture of assurance.

D.J. grinned, pleased with the turn of events. "That's what I like to hear. I think we've talked business long enough. I know you gentlemen are hungry. Let me take you out to a place where the food is good, the music is fabulous, and the women are spectacular."

The investors looked around, nodding in agreement, the mood now lighter and more relaxed.

Chapter 24
Meet And Mingle

The Miami Strip outside the clubs is alive with the pulse of neon lights and the hum of late-night activity. Inside the club, the atmosphere is electric, people lost in the rhythm of the music, bodies swaying to the beat.

In the VIP section, D.J., Hector, and a few investors sit comfortably while others mingle and dance, caught up in the energy of the night. Two beautiful women move sensually together on the dance floor, their chemistry undeniable.

Hector says, "I like the play, saying it was rival gangs. I think we got them hook, line, and sinker. Smooth."

Hector's eyes stay on the two women, and one of them notices, sending a flirtatious glance his way. The connection between them is magnetic.

D.J. responds, "We can't have Deamonotay interfere with what we're building. We have to hit him hard. We have to strategize this quickly. We've won back the confidence of the investors. We can't lose it again."

Hector agrees, "We'll get him. If he thinks that scare tactic with the semi is going to fuck us into a retreat, let me loose. I'll bring his head on a platter."

As the conversation continues, Hector's focus remains on the woman dancing. The chemistry between them only grows stronger as they share a heated gaze across the room.

D.J. shifts his attention from Hector to the dance floor, where some of the investors are letting loose, dancing with women, enjoying the fruits of their hard work. D.J. signals for the waitress to come over, ready to settle the bill. He stands up as she approaches, pulls out his card, and hands it to her with a polite nod. The waitress walks away.

One of the women from the dance floor catches the eye of the other and signals for her to join her. In the VIP section, the two women begin walking towards the table, their movements confident and deliberate. D.J. watches as they approach, intrigued by what the night may bring.

D.J. looks around, taking in the investors, sizing up the scene. "Well, it looks like our job here is done. These guys look well satisfied."

The women reach the VIP section but are halted by security. Hector signals to the security that they can come to him. The security lets them through. The women approach Hector and D.J.

One of the women says, "It looks like you guys are leaving."

Hector, still sitting, glances up at her. "Do you see me going anywhere?"

"Well, let me sit next to you then."

One of the women sits next to Hector, the other stands next to D.J., smiling.

D.J. smiles back. "This is Cindy. I'm Samantha."

"Hi, ladies. This is Hector. I'm D.J."

"Hi. We're looking for some guys tonight to show us a real good time. You guys look like those guys."

D.J. notices Samantha looking seductively at him. "We're definitely those guys."

Samantha's eyes light up. "Perfect. Let's turn it up."

Cindy cheers along, "Yes!"

D.J. gives them a polite but regretful smile. "Unfortunately, ladies, I have to take a rain check."

Cindy's face falls, surprised. "What?"

Hector interjects, raising a brow, "We're not going to..."

D.J. shakes his head. "No, you stay. I'm going to start preparing. I'll see you and Tomas tomorrow so we can start implementing. Ladies, I'm leaving you in safe hands. Hector here is nothing but a gentleman."

Cindy smirks, leaning closer. "Are you sure you can't stay? I may not want a gentleman tonight."

D.J. grins, eyes twinkling. "I wish I could, believe me. Well, man, it seems your hands are full tonight."

With a gentle gesture, he guides Cindy to sit beside Hector, then steps back. Hector nods confidently.

"I got it covered. I'll see you tomorrow."

They exchange a brief embrace before the waitress returns with D.J.'s receipt to sign. As he takes care of the bill, he adds, "I'll leave Manuel and Luis with you. I'll take the other two and the investors with me."

"Cool. I'll see you tomorrow," Hector replies, turning his attention back to the women as D.J. heads out.

Chapter 25
Surprise, Surprise

An expensive hotel overlooks the beach, its silhouette glowing warmly against the night sky. In the hallway outside two grand suite doors, Manuel and Luis stand guard, scanning for any sign of trouble.

Inside the suite, Hector lies sprawled on the bed, arms engulfed in the tantalizing touch of Samantha and Cindy, leaning in close, their mouths meeting his in heated, lingering kisses. The mood is charged, electric, as the three of them sink further into the bed, the women holding his gaze with a knowing intensity, their movements slow and deliberate.

As they rise, their hands slip to their dresses, sequins glinting under the dim lights. They ease the dresses off, revealing concealed pistols holstered high on their inner thighs, silencers already attached. With quick, practiced motions, they pull their weapons free and point them both at Hector, their gazes cold and methodical.

"Surprise, puta!" Cindy's voice cuts through the silence, her gun trained on him.

"Fuck." Hector's voice is tense, his eyes darting between the two women.

"Turn around." Cindy snaps, her stance steady and demanding.

Outside the suite, Manuel and Luis stand at their posts, their attention diverted as the door opens. Samantha stands there in a robe, her expression calm.

"Hey, guys. Hector is calling you." she says smoothly, motioning them inside.

The security guards enter the room with Samantha leading the way. She strides confidently in front of them, taking a sharp right into the bathroom. The guards catch sight of her slipping off her robe, preparing to step into the shower as the sound of water begins to fill the room.

Straight ahead, the security guards see Cindy, half-dressed, back turned, wearing only panties as she puts on her bra. The sight momentarily distracts them as they walk further into the room, but then they surprisingly see Hector hog-tied on the hotel floor. They quickly glance back at Cindy, who, with a playful smile, looks over her shoulder at them.

Before they have a chance to pull out their weapons, two compressed sounds from a silencer are heard as the bullets hit the backs of Manuel and Luis, causing them both to collapse, dead. Standing behind them, Samantha holds her nine-millimeter, her eyes briefly meeting Cindy's without saying a word.

Cindy picks up her cell phone and dials a number, her face calm and determined. "We got one of them ready for pickup," she says, then hangs up the phone.

Chapter 26

Deamonotay Confronts Hector

Hector hung suspended in the dim, oppressive confines of Deamonotay's torture room. His wrists and ankles were bound tightly, his body sagging with exhaustion. Samantha and Cindy stood nearby, their roles as silent sentinels unchanged.

The door swung open, and Deamonotay entered, his steps slow and deliberate, his expression a blend of satisfaction and disdain. He looked over at Hector, a cold smile creeping across his face.

"Hector. Hector." he called, his voice filled with twisted mockery. "The last we talked, you said you would give me what I was asking for. Huh? That's what you said."

Hector's head lifted slowly, his weary eyes meeting Deamonotay's with a flicker of defiance. "Don't get down on yourself that you got duped by them. They have taken down the best. Who can resist the beauty of two Haitian women?"

Hector's eyes shifted, narrowing as he looked more intensely at the women standing by. Deamonotay stepped closer, his tone dripping with a mix of mockery and conviction.

"Oh yes, Haitians!! You have your guard up when you see people of my hue, when the real villain looks like you." he gestured grandly, his voice softer now, almost reverent. "Our homeland is rich with different pigments. I could have had the assassins deal with you right there in the hotel room, but I wanted to meet you close and personal to let you know there is no door the devil can't enter."

Hector's gaze remained fixed on Deamonotay, his breath shallow. Deamonotay reached forward, grabbing Hector's face in a rough grip.

"I received some very depressing news that my top soldier, Mr. Grande, was found with a hole in his head."

Hector glared, his eyes steady, refusing to give any satisfaction in his expression. Deamonotay shook his head. "A magnificent soldier. I underestimated you all. I should have sent more men. I won't make that mistake again."

He stepped closer, his voice lowering to a dark murmur as he continued, "Grande and I, we'd use this room to get anything we wanted from people. We'd string up a hog right where you are now, make our guest watch, and then introduce the whip."

His hand moved to a case nearby, lifting a heavy, multi-tailed whip. Hector's gaze narrowed as he took in the sight of the brutal instrument, each leather tail gleaming under the dim light. His voice cut through the tension like a blade.

Deamonotay said, "Mr. Grande would start tearing off the flesh of that hog, meat everywhere, pouring down the drain, all over the person. By the time he was finished, we could ask them anything, and they would tell it."

Deamonotay's voice grew cold and deliberate as he addressed the room. "My friend is not here, and neither is a hog. Ladies, step out the door as Hector plays the hog and I play Mr. Grande."

His gaze locked onto Hector's, both men staring at each other intensely. Without a word, the two assassins silently obeyed, stepping out of the room and closing the door behind them.

Deamonotay turned away. "I'm amazed," the voice taunted. "All this time I've spoken, you haven't said a word."

Hector slowly raised his head, his expression unwavering. "If today is the day I go, you holding me up, motherfucker."

The room seemed to still for a moment, the words hanging heavy in the air. Then a slow, predatory smile spread across the face of his captor.

"Ah touche," came the low reply, as Deamonotay draped himself in a protective covering before reaching for the whip, its braided length a symbol of pain and power.

"Like I said," the voice echoed through the room, chilling and resolute, "...this room is for extracting information. I just want to extract from you a pound of flesh or more."

The whip snapped through the air, raised high before descending with brutal force. A scream tore from Hector's throat, raw and anguished. The impact reverberated, the splatter painting the space in stark, violent strokes.

The relentless sound of the whip cracked through the air, accompanied by Hector's anguished screams echoing through the cold walls of the torture room. The whip's steady rhythm continued, its merciless strikes a grim soundtrack to the unfolding torment.

Outside the door, Cindy and Samantha stood silently. The faint light from the corridor cast shadows across their faces as they exchanged a glance. Even they were set back as they heard Hector's demise.

Chapter 27
Are We Ready

The atmosphere in the dimly lit warehouse garage buzzed with quiet intensity. Daniel sat in the back of a black van, the side door wide open, fine-tuning a complex piece of software. The van was filled with what looked like three large computer screens, all integrated into one centralized system, and the glow of multiple monitors displaying streams of data.

Deamonotay stepped into the room, wiping his hands clean with a small towel, a residual reminder of Hector's demise still on his fingers.

"Brother, are you ready for phase three?" Deamonotay asked, his voice cutting through the mechanical ambiance.

Daniel didn't look up, his fingers dancing over the keyboard.

"Everybody is in place." he replied, his tone as focused as his work. "I'm finalizing the operations now. We'll be ready for tomorrow night."

"Good." Deamonotay said, pausing briefly as he tossed the towel aside. "I don't want you going inside. No matter what happens, you operate everything from a perimeter. Okay?"

Daniel nodded, his focus still on the screen.

"No problem."

Deamontay repeats his command with authority. "I'm serious! Only the perimeter!" Daniel finally lifts up his head and looks at his brother. "I hear you...perimeter!"

Satisfied, Deamonotay turned and left the lab, the faint sound of his footsteps disappearing down the hallway. As Daniel continued his preparations, the glow of the monitors reflected in his eyes, a quiet determination mirrored in his expression.

Chapter 28

Where Is Hector

D.J. sat in his opulent office, the phone pressed to his ear, his frustration evident as he tried to reach Hector. "Come on, pick up." he muttered, drumming his fingers on the desk. The sound of the office doors opening diverted his attention. Tomas and Rosa entered, and D.J.'s face lit up as he quickly hung up the phone and rose to greet them.

"Rosa, oh my God. Look at you!" he exclaimed, crossing the room with hurried steps. He pulled them both into a heartfelt embrace, holding on as if to reassure himself they were truly there. "Hey, what did the doctor say?"

"Bruised ribs," Rosa replied, her tone matter-of-fact despite the exhaustion on her face. "No concussion. Pain pills that can numb a moose."

D.J. shook his head, concern etched on his features.

Meanwhile, three large charter buses and two vans emblazoned with the logo "Flamingo Touring" rode up to the security booth of D.J.'s gated community, where affluent people and even stars resided. The gleaming vehicles looked ordinary enough, but their arrival disrupted the stillness of the night.

A security guard stepped out of the booth, clipboard in hand, waving his arms to signal the approaching buses to stop. The engines idled as the vehicles came to a halt. The guard walked to the lead bus, his expression stern but polite as he addressed the driver.

"It's after hours for touring," he said firmly. "You're going to have to turn back around and show them the rest of the city. Come back tomorrow."

The bus driver nodded, acknowledging the guard's words with a neutral expression. For a brief moment, it seemed the encounter would end uneventfully. Then, in a swift, shocking motion, the driver pulled a pistol from beneath his jacket and fired a single shot. The sharp crack echoed through the air as the guard crumpled to the ground, lifeless.

The charter bus door hissed open, and another man stepped out—a hulking figure clad in dark clothing, his face unreadable. Without hesitation, he dragged the guard's body out of sight, stepped into the booth, and assumed the dead man's post. He pressed a button, and the gate began to slide open.

The buses and vans rolled forward, their engines rumbling ominously as they entered the residential community.

Inside D.J.'s mansion, the atmosphere was markedly different. D.J. gently guided Rosa to one of the plush chairs in his office. Rosa hesitated, clearly unused to people helping her, but D.J. insisted.

"Sit, my niec.," he said softly, his concern evident.

Rosa finally relented, lowering herself into the chair with a mixture of exhaustion and reluctance. Tomas stood nearby, his eyes scanning the room while D.J. remained standing, his worry still lingering.

Rosa adjusted herself in her chair, brushing off the concern with a dismissive wave. "I'm good. I'm good." she insisted.

D.J. turned his attention to Tomas, his brow furrowed with worry. "Tomas, you?"

"I'm good." Tomas replied, settling into his seat. "Grande was built like a tank. He kept coming," Tomas said, shaking his head as if still in disbelief.

D.J. leaned back in his chair at the desk, exhaling sharply. "And you were able to walk away from it. You lucky sons of a bitch. We have a major shipment coming in. Also, we can't have any further disturbance at any of our sites. I have a plan of attack for revenge. Putting their hands on my niece, on my family, my Tiffany! He must pay!" He paused, his gaze narrowing as he asked, "Have you seen Hector?"

Tomas and Rosa exchanged glances, shaking their heads in unison. "No," they both responded.

Tomas added, "I've been calling, but no answer."

Outside the community, the charter buses and vans cruised slowly through the quiet community streets, their headlights slicing through the dark. They came across a community police officer parked on the side of the road. The caravan came to a gradual halt, the engines humming low.

The police officer, noticing the unusual activity, furrowed his brow and reached for his radio. His eyes narrowed at the sight of the late-night touring caravan.

"What are they doing so late?" he muttered to himself, lifting the radio to his lips. "Security," the officer said firmly into the device, "why is someone touring after hours?"

A moment of static crackled through the line before the security guard's voice came through, sounding calm and matter-of-fact. "Their plane came in late. They paid for the late tour."

The officer frowned, his face reflecting disbelief. His gaze shifted back to the caravan, clearly unsatisfied with the explanation. One of the tinted windows of the charter bus slid open, the nozzle of a rifle with a silencer emerging, aiming toward the police car parked on the side of the road. The rifle fired. Bullets pierced the front glass. The police officer slumped over, dead.

The charter bus door opened, and two goons sprinted out, heading directly to the police car. They pulled open the driver's side door, dragged the police officer's body out, and shoved it into the seat. The goons climbed into the front seats of the car, started the engine, and maneuvered the vehicle in front of the caravan. The police car now led the buses and vans deeper into the gated community, heading straight for D.J.'s mansion.

Inside the mansion, D.J. leaned back in his chair. "I left him last night with a couple of women."

"You did?" Tomas asked, raising an eyebrow.

"Yeah," D.J. replied with a slight grin. "I knew he was going to have a good time, but he understood the seriousness of this matter. He said he'd be here."

Rosa leaned forward, shaking her head. "Hector can't resist anything with high heels."

Tomas smirked, "He'll show up."

Outside, the police car stopped the caravan down the street from D.J.'s mansion. The two goons in the police car jumped out and ran back to one of the charter buses. Two more goons jumped out of each van. One goon opened the side of one van, revealing Daniel sitting in a gaming chair in front of a high-tech computerized system with three monitors.

"I'm knocking out cellular service for a perimeter of 800 feet," Daniel announced, his hands working quickly over the controls. A small cone antenna was shown on top of the van. The computer monitor inside the van displayed the perimeter shutting off the cellular service.

"It's off." Daniel confirmed.

The other goon opened the back doors of the other van. Inside, there was a large drone and hundreds of smaller drones stacked and ready for deployment. At Daniel's van, the goon tapped the van to signal him to go.

"Turning on master drone." Daniel said. The master drone lit up. The computer screen showed the big drone's camera, and then the drone lifted up, leaving the van, soaring above D.J.'s mansion.

Meanwhile, inside the mansion, D.J. wondered, "What's this? Yacht excursion? Secret rendezvous? Niece, did you get permission to see this man?" Turning his question to Tomas. Tomas and Rosa exchanged glances, and D.J. burst into laughter.

"No!" D.J. said, wiping away his mirth. "I think you chose well. I like what I see. We should toast to this. This is special. Let me go to my collection and pick something."

Meanwhile, the big drone's camera continued to survey the area. Daniel's computer monitor highlighting the positions of the guards scattered across the property. The small drones swarmed over D.J.'s property, their quiet hum the only sound as they silently navigated the night air.

The first guard barely has time to react before a drone crashes into him, sending a sharp burst of light and sound into the quiet of the estate. The explosions are precise—compressed, deadly bursts. As the guards are struck down, one by one, their bodies crumple to the ground under the relentless assault of the drones.

Inside a nearby van, Daniel sits with eyes locked on the screens before him. His fingers move with calculated precision as he targets each of DJ's guards, marking their positions on a digital map. One by one, the monitors highlight their locations, each signal blinking red before fading.

Overhead, a larger drone takes flight, capturing a wide aerial view of the estate and feeding high-resolution imagery back to Daniel's console. The coordinated ambush unfolds with brutal efficiency.

Meanwhile, inside the mansion, DJ grows uneasy. He glances around, tension building.

"Keep calling Hector," he says. "See where that loco is at."

Oblivious to the chaos unfolding outside, unaware that his security is being systematically dismantled, Tomas pulls out his phone and glances at the screen. He tries to call Hector, but the service is acting up—no signal. His brow furrows.

Meanwhile, outside, the few remaining guards begin to sense something is off. They look around, noticing the absence of their fellow men at key posts.

But it's already too late.The small aerial drone strikes with deadly precision, eliminating the guards one by one in sharp, controlled explosions.Inside, Tomas suddenly stands. A wave of unease crashes over him. He starts pacing the room.

"I don't like this," he mutters, glancing at his phone again.

"No reception."

Chapter 29

Mansion Murders

Haitian goons dressed in all black pour out of the charter buses. They open the luggage compartments, revealing large cases filled with guns. Each of the approximately 90 goons is handed a weapon with silent efficiency. They begin scaling the walls of D.J.'s mansion.

Inside the mansion, Rosa stands abruptly and walks over to the walkie-talkie on D.J.'s desk.

"Team, let us know when you have a visual on Hector." Rosa says, her tone firm.

As she waits for a response, there is only silence. Rosa frowns and repeats, "Team, do you hear me? When you have a visual on Hector, let us know."

Tomas's eyes dart toward the security screens. He studies one monitor, then another, his concern growing with each glance.

"Where is the team?" Tomas mutters, his voice tinged with unease. He leans in, scanning every screen. One shows the yard outside, empty. Another screen displays an equally desolate view of the perimeter. His tension escalates as his eyes lock onto a feed showing the wine collection room.

There, D.J. moves casually, oblivious to the unfolding chaos. D.J. opens the wine collection doors downstairs, steps inside, and begins browsing the racks. He studies several bottles before settling on one, holding it up for inspection with a look of satisfaction.

Back in the office, Tomas's attention snaps to the screen as movement flickers in the corner of the feed. D.J. closes the door only to find two goons suddenly in his path, their presence catching him off guard. Without hesitation, he hurls the wine bottle at the closest one. The glass shatters on impact, sending the goon stumbling backward into the one behind him, both momentarily thrown off balance.

Without missing a beat, D.J. seizes the fallen goon's weapon and fires, taking out both intruders.

"D.J.!" Tomas yells.

Three more goons burst into the wine collection area, guns blazing. Bullets ricochet off the walls, shattering bottles and sending shards of glass flying. D.J. dives for cover, quickly retaliating with precise shots. His aim is sharp and unrelenting, dropping two of the goons. In the chaos, he fails to notice another goon slipping into the collection area and positioning himself behind him. The goon strikes D.J. on the back of his neck with his weapon, the impact rendering him unconscious. The two goons grab D.J. and drag him out of the mansion.

Rosa immediately looks at the screen and sees the goons dragging D.J. away. She quickly runs over to a button underneath D.J.'s desk and pushes it. A wall opens up, revealing an assortment of different types of guns. Rosa and Tomas run to the assortment of guns. Rosa tosses Tomas two guns as she grabs two for herself.

Tomas and Rosa rush out of the office to help D.J. As they start running down the stairs, an explosion erupts at the mansion's front and side doors. The blast shakes the foundation of the house, sending dust and debris into the air. The force of the explosion throws them off balance for a moment, but they quickly recover, their eyes narrowing as they hear the sound of gunfire approaching.

An extremely large group of goons marches through the entrances, guns raised, and starts shooting at Tomas and Rosa. The air fills with the deafening sound of gunfire as Tomas and Rosa immediately return fire, ducking behind pillars for cover. The goons continue to fire relentlessly, forcing Tomas and Rosa to stay low. A bullet grazes Tomas's arm, pain shooting through him, but he grits his teeth and stays focused.

They both know more of Deamonotay's goons are steadily advancing up the stairs, getting closer. Rosa looks at Tomas, her voice tense with urgency.

"We have to go back to the office!"

Tomas and Rosa notice one of the goons downstairs has a small rocket launcher and starts to point it at them. Tomas grabs Rosa's arm and pulls her back toward the office.

"Let's go!" Tomas shouts.

Tomas and Rosa run back to the office. As they reach the door, Rosa attempts to close it behind them, but before she can, the goon fires the rocket launcher. The explosion blasts through the office door, sending shockwaves through the room. The force of the blast knocks Tomas and Rosa off their feet, throwing them backward. Debris fills the air, and the entire office is consumed by smoke and chaos.

The explosion leaves both of them dazed, barely conscious. Rosa feels pain coursing through her body, but she forces herself to focus through the thick smoke. She looks up. Everything on the desk has been blown off, scattered across the room in pieces. Her gaze darts around, searching for the remote that opens the secret door—a means of escape—but it's nowhere to be seen.

Tomas shakes off the daze and hurries over to Rosa, his voice urgent though tinged with concern.

"Rosa, are you okay?"

Dazed but determined, Rosa slowly gets to her feet. She stumbles but manages to make her way back to the assortment of guns.

"Knock over the desk," she orders, her voice sharp with focus. "The top is solid steel. We might have to make a stand. Find the remote so we can get out of here."

Tomas races to the desk, searching frantically. He doesn't find the remote, so he topples the desk, hoping the movement will reveal something. Rosa, already moving with purpose, grabs assault weapons and ammunition, tossing them to Tomas. As she prepares for the fight, she picks up an assault rifle for herself, her expression hardening.

Suddenly, the sound of gunfire erupts as the goons outside the office door start shooting through it. Rosa immediately returns fire, her aim true as she takes out several of the intruders. Tomas joins in, his shots keeping the attackers at bay. The goons fall one by one, but the fight only grows more intense. A regiment of armed men lines both sides of the wide accordion-style staircase leading up to the office, each one ready to unleash a brutal end for Tomas and Rosa.

Rosa drops into a crouch behind the desk, her instincts sharper than ever, already anticipating their next move. Her heart pounds—finding the remote is absolutely critical. Then there it is.

She grabs it in her hand, but just as she does, more goons flood into the office, weapons raised and firing. Tomas ducks low behind the desk as well seeing the barrage coming forth.

"So you've come for a big kiss?" Rosa taunts, her voice dripping with menace. "Let me give you a big kiss!"

With a fierce grin, she punches in a code and presses a button on the remote. Instantly, red lights flash on each step of the staircase outside the office doors. A split second later, a massive explosion rocks the mansion—obliterating the left staircase and taking out every goon caught on it.

One of the main goons at the front motions for another to bring him a vest with smoke spray canisters. The main goon takes one of the canisters off the vest, removes the clip, and throws it into the office. Moments later, the room begins to fill with thick smoke, clouding the air.

Rosa opens the escape room door behind the bookshelf with the remote. She drops the remote and then picks up her automatic weapon.

"Go!" Rosa commands.

Tomas runs as Rosa springs up, instantly engaging in a hail of gunfire toward the goons in the office. Tomas dashes into the secret escape room behind the bookshelf. The goons return fire, forcing Rosa to retreat behind the desk for cover. More goons rush into the office, quickly taking cover as well.

"I've got you covered!" Tomas calls from the escape room.

Rosa slips the remote into her pocket, grabs her weapon, and tries to make a run for the escape room. Tomas continues to shoot at the goons, trying to suppress their advance. However, the relentless barrage of bullets from the goons is overwhelming. One of the bullets clips Rosa's calf. The pain shoots through her, but she keeps moving. Rosa falls to the floor, her body weakening from the gunshot wound. She drags herself back to D.J.'s desk, seeking whatever protection it can offer.

Tomas, furious and determined, begins firing wildly, unloading everything his automatic weapon has to offer. But soon, the click of an empty chamber signals the end of his clip.

"Damn!" he curses under his breath, dropping the spent weapon to the floor. Without hesitation, he reaches for another gun strapped to his back.

"Come on, baby! Get in here!" Tomas shouts, his voice a mix of urgency and defiance as he continues the fight to protect Rosa and himself.

Rosa grits her teeth, summoning every last bit of strength. She drops her automatic weapon and begins to crawl, dragging her injured body toward the escape room. Tomas is engaged in a furious exchange of gunfire with the goons, bullets flying all around them. Then another shot lands in Rosa's side. She cries out in pain, her body collapsing to the floor. She rolls back toward D.J.'s desk, using it for cover once again.

Tomas is quickly running out of options as his gun clicks empty.

"Damn!" he curses again, his heart racing. He looks around frantically, but there's nothing else to grab. No more weapons, no more ammunition. His eyes lock on Rosa, who is now lying face down, her body barely moving, badly hurt.

"Rosa! You hear me?" Tomas shouts, desperation rising in his voice.

Rosa, battered and barely conscious, pushes herself up slowly, lifting her head. The fight isn't over yet.

Rosa's body trembles as she turns, resting against D.J.'s desk. The pain from her wound is unbearable, but she forces herself to focus on Tomas. She cries out, the agony consuming her for a moment before she tries to steady herself.

Tomas's voice is frantic, urging her to keep going.

"Baby, throw me the weapon so I can cover you! Throw me the weapon!"

Rosa's hand slowly rises to her side, her fingers trembling. She looks down and sees it stained with blood. Her expression softens, and she looks at Tomas, her voice turning somber, barely a whisper.

"Tell Tiffany mommy loves her. You make sure you tell her."

Tomas's face tightens with panic.

"Don't look at the blood. Look at me. Throw me the gun!"

The air is thick with the sound of gunfire as the goons outside press forward, their shots relentless. Rosa glances up, peeking around the desk. She sees them pushing into the office, steadily closing in.

Tomas is desperate now, his eyes locked on her.

"Throw me the gun, woman!"

Rosa's gaze meets Tomas's, the weight of the moment sinking in. Her fingers brush the remote in her pocket, and Tomas watches her, unsure of what she's planning. Every second counts, but Rosa's next move could change everything.

Tomas watches in disbelief as Rosa presses the button on the remote. The escape door begins to close automatically, and he's helplessly pushed back.

"What are you doing? What are you doing, Rosa?"

With a calm yet somber expression, she meets his gaze.

"Loving you."

As the door slowly moves, Tomas struggles, trying to hold it open, but it's too powerful. The weight of the door forces him back, and despite his efforts, it closes with a decisive finality. He slams his hands against the door, shouting as it seals shut between them.

"Rosa! Rosa!"

Tomas pushes against the door with all his strength, but it refuses to budge. His eyes dart around, desperately searching for a lever or anything that could reopen it, but there is nothing. Frustrated, he slams his fists against the door in disgust.

"I'm coming for you. I'll go back around, you hear me?"

His breath quickens as he turns and spots the pole leading down into the escape tunnel. In a panic, he wraps his hands around it and starts to slide.

"D.J., show me the way. Come on."

He slides down the pole, his shoes hitting the floor of the tunnel with a thud. As soon as his feet make contact, the lights along the escape route flicker on, illuminating the entire path leading out of the mansion grounds.

Tomas glances ahead, spotting the BMW waiting for him, but his attention is quickly drawn to something on the security screen mounted in the tunnel. He rushes to the screen, his heart racing. He sees the office, and behind the desk, Rosa, vulnerable and exposed. The goons are closing in, making their way into the office.

Tomas's eyes widen in horror.

"No!"

Rosa throws down the remote with a determined look, her hands quickly reaching for her automatic weapon. She scans the floor and finds a single magazine, reloading her gun with swift precision. She speaks from behind the desk, her voice cold but full of fury.

"Let me introduce you to the Black Widow and spin my web."

Rosa rises from behind the desk, firing her weapon with deadly accuracy. Goons fall one after another, but soon the magazine runs dry. She looks down at the floor, searching for another clip, but finds nothing. She stands her ground, staring defiantly at the advancing goons.

The head goon, hearing the silence, motions for the others to move. In a wave, about 20 goons flood the office, weapons raised, their eyes locked on Rosa. With her head raised high, she shows no fear, no longer hiding, but standing strong behind D.J.'s desk. She meets their gaze, unflinching.

The main goon steps forward, surveying the scene. The bodies of his fallen comrades lie scattered across the office. He looks up at Rosa, nodding a silent acknowledgment of her defiance. Without a word, he turns and signals for the goons to fire.

In an instant, the office erupts in gunfire. The goons unleash a barrage of bullets in Rosa's direction. The main goon stands at the doorway with his back to the chaos, his figure illuminated by the flashes of gunfire.

The sound of gunfire continues to echo.

The Black Widow has fallen.

Rosa does not rise again.

Her body lies motionless behind the desk as the main goon steps out of the office, leaving the destruction behind him.

Rosa is dead.

Chapter 30
The Getaway Payback

Tomas stares at the security screen, his body rigid as the realization sinks in. His face twists in anguish, and a cry bursts from him. "Rosa!" His voice echoes in the tunnel, but there's no one to hear him. Overwhelmed, he stumbles back, his legs giving way. As he slides down the side of the BMW, he collapses, sitting on the ground with his hands covering his face.

As tears flow freely, he suddenly sees a flash image of his mother, Elizabeth, her voice echoing in his mind: "Don't be like your father." Her trembling voice is full of pain and loss.

"Damn you!" he shouts, his voice filled with rage. His chest heaves with heavy, shuddering breaths. Slowly, he pulls his hands away from his face, his fingers slick with tears. He tilts his head back, resting it against the cold metal of the BMW. For a moment, there is only the sound of his ragged, broken breathing. Then something shifts in him. His breathing steadies, and his jaw tightens.

"You fucked with the wrong one." he says, his voice low and filled with menace. He pauses, his teary eyes now sharp and focused, staring straight ahead as if seeing his enemies through the steel of the tunnel. His words are quiet: "A lot of families will weep tonight."

The weight of his resolve in the air, Tomas struggles to pick himself up, his body heavy with grief and rage. Slowly, he makes his way to the driver's side door of the BMW. His gaze shifts to the wall, where a small selection of guns gleams under the dim tunnel lights. Without hesitation, Tomas begins grabbing each weapon along with a bag of ammunition, tossing them into the car with purposeful movements.

Reaching the console, he presses a button marked "Entrance Open." The light beside it turns green, signaling the tunnel's outer exit is now accessible. Tomas climbs into the driver's seat, his hands trembling as he picks up one of the guns and checks its chamber. It is loaded. He places it on the passenger seat and starts the car, the engine roaring to life. The BMW shoots down the tunnel at high speed, the opening ahead already parting, camouflaged by dense, high bushes.

Meanwhile, back at the front of D.J.'s mansion, two goons drag D.J.'s unconscious body toward a black van parked nearby. One of them calls out with a sinister grin, "We got D.J.."

Daniel remains focused. "Good. Take him in the other van to Deamonotay," Daniel orders, but still glued to his console.

The two goons drag D.J. to the other van. They grab zip ties from the van, binding D.J.'s wrists and ankles tightly before sliding the door shut. Meanwhile, Tomas' BMW roars through the camouflaged tunnel opening, crashing through the high bushes onto the golf course.

"Can't leave you! Coming D.J.!" he mutters under his breath, spinning the car in a hard turn to head toward the mansion's front drive.

The van's engine rumbles to life just as the goons finish securing D.J. in the back. One climbs into the driver's seat, only to freeze at the sight of Tomas's headlights slicing through the dark.

A goon replies, "Someone's coming!"

The other goons near Daniel's van spin toward the oncoming vehicle, raising their weapons.

Daniel's voice cuts through the tense air. "Shoot that car!"

The goons outside start firing at Tomas. A couple of the goons drop to the ground. However the goons in the van, who were trying to leave, instead duck inside the van to avoid the gunfire.

Tomas stops the car in the middle of the street, gets out, and uses it for cover. The goons and Tomas exchange bullets, the sound of gunfire echoing in the air. Tomas keeps firing, taking down the goons one by one in the street.

All of a sudden, a goon emerges from behind Daniel's van and starts firing. Tomas stays low, continuing to take cover behind the BMW. Then, in one swift motion, Tomas springs out, firing relentlessly. His bullets rip through the air and riddle the van, finally hitting the goon. Tomas watches as the goon crumples to the ground.

Tomas runs toward the van, hoping to rescue D.J. When he cautiously opens the sliding door, his heart sinks. D.J. is nowhere to be found. Instead, Tomas is taken aback by the sight of Daniel, drenched in blood, his lifeless body slumped from the bullets that went through the van.

Frustration takes hold of Tomas as he looks around, realizing that D.J. is not there. He quickly moves around the van, searching for any sign of where they might've taken him. Meanwhile, the two goons in the other van with D.J. catches sight of the bullet-riddled van of Daniel and tense up.

"I think he killed Daniel! Get out of here!" one shouts.

The van's engine roars to life, and it screeches down the street, tires spinning on the asphalt. Tomas watches as the other van speeds off in the opposite direction, a sinking feeling in his gut. He clenches his jaw, his mind racing.

"That must be the van that took D.J.!" he mutters, his fists clenching in frustration, knowing he's just missed his chance to save D.J.

Chapter 31

The Hunt Is On

Tomas slams his foot on the gas, the BMW roaring down the street as he chases after the van. His hands grip the steering wheel tightly, knuckles white. With the intensity of his focus, the van ahead of him swerves in and out of traffic, but Tomas matches its pace, determined not to lose sight of it.

Remembering he needs to warn Hector, he dials Hector's number. The phone rings, but instead of Hector's voice, he hears the familiar voicemail.

"Dammit, pick up the phone!" Tomas curses under his breath, frustration boiling over. "Hector, don't go to D.J.'s. Where are you? We got hit hard. We lost the whole team. We lost Rosa..."

Tomas's voice cracks, the weight of the loss hitting him like a physical blow. He swallows hard, his breaths shaky as he continues.

"Look! They got D.J. I'm following them. When you get this, track my phone. I think they're taking him to Deamonotay. We can get them there. Call me back."

With that, Tomas hangs up, his mind reeling from everything that's happened, but he pushes it aside, focusing all of his energy on the road ahead. He can't afford to think about anything other than rescuing D.J.

Tomas hangs up the phone. Meanwhile, Deamonotay is on the phone with the two goons.

"Good. Bring him here." Deamonotay commands. "And let Tomas follow. Where's Daniel?"

The goon in the van pauses, sensing the tension in Deamonotay's voice.

Deamonotay immediately picks up on the pause, his anger rising. "Pierre, where's my brother?" he demands, his voice seething.

The goon in the van takes a deep breath, reluctant to answer but eventually responds quickly, knowing the danger in angering Deamonotay further.

"Deamonotay... Tomas was shooting up the van. I don't think Daniel—" the goon trails off, not daring to finish the sentence.

Deamonotay lets out a horrific scream, the sound echoing through the room, his rage palpable. He quickly hangs up the phone and calls Daniel's number, his hands trembling as the cell rings endlessly.

"Pick up. Pick up. Pick up!"

Deamonotay's voice is frantic, but the phone goes to voicemail. A guttural scream erupts from his chest, filled with raw anguish and fury. His hands shake as he drops the phone to the floor, the sound of it clattering like a final toll. He staggers backward, bracing himself on his desk, his head bowed in utter defeat.

Meanwhile, the van arrives at Deamonotay's torture facility. The two goons exit the van and drag the bound D.J. from the back, his body limp but beginning to stir as he regains consciousness.

From a block away, Tomas watches the scene unfold, his eyes narrowing in focus. He parks the BMW quietly, keeping a low profile as he observes the goons hauling D.J. inside. Tomas slips from the car, scanning his surroundings carefully. His heart pounds with purpose as he loads up on as many weapons as he can carry, also grabbing a high-tech rifle.

Inside the facility, the two goons drag D.J. to the back office. They tie him to a chair with brutal efficiency.

Deamonotay strides into the room before placing a cat o' nine tails case onto his desk. The faint clink of the case's contents speaks of the horrors soon to unfold. His cold eyes fix on the bound D.J.

"I got something for you." he sneers. "But first, I'm going to deal with your boy Tomas."

He leans down and smacks D.J. on the head. "If I can't have the properties, neither will you."

His attention is drawn to the security screen. He smirks as he sees Tomas cautiously stepping into the storefront entrance, his weapon drawn, eyes scanning the room.

"Just like a fly getting caught in the web," Deamonotay mutters.

Tomas moves carefully through the dusty storefront, his instincts sharp as he searches for any clue as to where they had taken D.J. His sharp eyes land on a door at the back of the store, slightly ajar. He approaches it, his grip on his weapon tightening.

In his office, Deamonotay presses the button on his desk's PA system. His voice echoes through the space.

"Come on in, Tomas. I left the door open for you."

Tomas cautiously steps inside the door to the torture room, his gun at the ready.

Deamonotay's voice continues, smug and calm. "As I was explaining to D.J.—no properties for me, no properties for him. There are consequences for not working with me."

In his office, Deamonotay lowers the microphone to address the goon standing near the door, his tone sharp and commanding.

"Go down there and handle him."

Without hesitation, the goon sprints out. Deamonotay, unbothered, returns to the microphone. His words drip with malice.

"With D.J., I'm going to take his life and take his land. But with you, Tomas, I've got something even more special planned."

Tomas grits his teeth, gripping his weapon tighter. The tension in the air thickens as he prepares for whatever lay ahead.

Deamonotay's voice echoes through the room, laced with cruel certainty. "With D.J., his life now belongs to me, and soon, his land. But with you? I think it's fitting. Since you took my brother, I present to you someone who I guess you deemed as a brother."

Tomas steps into the torture room, his breath catching as he takes in the horrific sight of Hector's mangled body. His mouth opens in shock. A wave of complete numbness overtakes him as he steps closer to Hector's lifeless form. Wearing an expression of disgust and sorrow, he leans his head against the side of Hector's hanging body.

On a nearby security screen, Deamonotay watches Tomas's anguish unfold with grim satisfaction.

"Your brother—gone. My brother—gone. I guess that makes you and me brothers. But not for long, though. My men are coming back as we speak...but I'll take care of you before they come back."

The two goons step cautiou sly into the torture room, their eyes scanning the dimly lit space. They don't notice Tomas. Suddenly, a shot rings out, and one of the goon's bodies is flung into the air, crashing to the ground with a thud.

The other goon turns and sees Tomas. Without wasting a moment, he starts firing. The two exchange shots back and forth, each ducking and moving to avoid the deadly barrage. Then, the goon is hit and falls to the ground, his body crumpling as he collapses.

Tomas approaches the goon, his footsteps heavy and deliberate. Without hesitation, he finishes him off, ensuring there is no further threat.

Chapter 32
The Scar Begins

Tomas hears Deamonotay's voice echo through the PA system.

"Come and get D.J. before I do."

Tomas clenches his jaw, his fury evident.

"I'm coming, motherfucker," he growls.

He opens the back door of the torture room, stepping cautiously into the next space. It's another large room filled with raw materials stacked haphazardly. The dim lighting casts eerie shadows, offering very little visibility in the distance. Tomas spots Deamonotay's office. The door is ajar, and a faint light trickles out, cutting through the darkness. Determined but wary, Tomas moves toward the office. He stays low, ducking behind the raw materials, his eyes scanning every inch of the space. He knows all too well—this could be a trap.

He edges closer to the office, his heart pounding with each silent step. Tomas believes this is where D.J. and Deamonotay are waiting. He presses his back against the cold, unforgiving wall just outside the door, the air thick with tension. Taking a steadying breath, he raises his nickel-plated weapon close to his face, his grip firm and ready. His eyes flick to the slight crack in the door, scanning for any sign of movement as he prepares to make his move.

Suddenly, a red dot appears on the surface of his nickel-plated weapon, its glow sharp and unmissable. Tomas freezes, his breath hitching. He quickly glances toward the direction he believes the laser is coming from, his mind racing. His eyes strain to pick out details in the dim light, and he catches the faint outline of what he thinks is a rifle aimed at him. Before he can react further, the laser dot shifts, sliding from his weapon to his face. His chest tightens as he realizes the deadly precision now targeting him directly.

"What the—"

But before he can finish, his eyes widen in alarm. The red laser is fixed on him. He turns his head abruptly just as the sound of a gunshot rips through the air.

Deamonotay has fired.

Tomas pulls back, but not quickly enough. He is struck deep through the left cheek. It's a grazing wound, but the force is so strong it knocks him off his feet, sending him crashing into some raw materials.

Deamonotay, convinced Tomas is dead but driven by the need for certainty, grabs his weapon from his back and then picks up the cat o' nine tails. His fingers curl around its handle as he starts walking toward Tomas, who lies motionless. Then abruptly, coming from out of the raw materials, a shot rings out, striking Deamonotay with a force that causes him to stagger. The impact sends a shock of pain through his body, and he recoils instinctively, clutching at his side where the bullet tore through. He drops his weapon, the force of the shot pushing him back and spinning him around until he crashes to one knee.

Tomas springs out of the raw materials, his weapon raised, pointing directly at Deamonotay. His finger tightens on the trigger, but the shot misses—the bullet grazing the air just past Deamonotay's shoulder.

Deamonotay bends down, turns around to face Tomas, and falls to the ground with the cat o' nine tails still in his hand. He swings it upward. Skin is torn as the whip makes contact with Tomas's hand.

Tomas groans in pain, clutching his injured hand instinctively as blood seeps between his fingers.

Deamonotay springs up with fiery rage, his movement sharp and aggressive. He swings the whip ferociously, the claws slicing through the air with menacing speed clinch Tomas' back. Tomas spins around and breaks into a run, desperation driving each hurried step. He rushes Deamonotay, and they collide in a violent struggle.

Tomas gains the upper hand, pinning Deamonotay to the ground, pressing his advantage. But then, Deamonotay grips the whip still attached to Tomas's back. With a sharp yank, the whip pulls, and Tomas screams in agony as the pain sears through him. He falls back, clutching his wound as Deamonotay struggles to catch his breath, sprawled on the floor beneath him.

Tomas, wracked with pain, struggles to get to his hands and knees. He looks up through blurred vision and spots a nearby pillar. With sheer determination, he pushes himself up, his legs unsteady as he staggers toward it. Reaching the pillar, he turns his back to it, wincing as the whip still clings to his flesh. With a grunt, he begins to slam his back against the pillar, each hit sending waves of agony through him. Finally, with a painful jerk, the whip loosens and falls to the ground, its claws no longer embedded in his skin.

Deamonotay struggles to rise from the ground. His eyes scan the room, settling on his weapon not too far from the office door. He looks at Tomas, a cold, cruel smile creeping across his face.

"I want you to hear what I do to D.J.!" Deamonotay sneers.

He staggers toward his weapon, struggling with each step. Tomas, in pain but determined, picks up the whip from the floor and pushes through the agony, rushing toward Deamonotay. But Deamonotay, now armed, strides over to the door of his office with a menacing mission. He opens it wide and steps inside, aiming his weapon at the tied-up D.J.

Deamonotay hears a voice from behind.

"Maybe God can give you property in the gates of hell."

Tomas, with all his might, swings the cat o' nine tails at Deamonotay's face. The claws of the whip stretch out and take hold of Deamonotay's cheek like a metal web. Then, Tomas flings the whip with both hands and pulls back with all his strength, eliciting a horrific scream of agony from Deamonotay. The whip, unforgivingly rigid, refuses to release as Tomas yanks it back. With immense force, the yank forces Deamonotay's head to snap back, catapulting him off his feet. He slams onto a nearby work table before collapsing onto the floor, losing his weapon.

Tomas lets go of the whip to search for the weapon Deamonotay dropped. Writhing in excruciating pain, with blood in his eyes and immobilized by the claws embedded in his face, Deamonotay realizes he's powerless to retaliate. Tomas finds the weapon and swiftly raises it, aiming at where Deamonotay should be—only to find the spot empty. His eyes dart left and right as he shifts the weapon, scanning the room.

Deamonotay has vanished. Nowhere to be found.

He's left the office.

D.J. looks at Tomas, his voice steady but pointed.

"It seems you're getting accustomed to having blood on your hands."

Shaking his head, Tomas looks down and notices blood dripping from his hands—a grim reminder of what is required to live this life.

"Let me get you out of here before the rest of Deamonotay's guys come," Tomas says, already releasing D.J. from his bindings. "We gotta grab Hector's body."

D.J. now realizing Hector is dead echoes his name,.... "Hector...?" Tomas confirms with a nod.

He carefully helps D.J. out of the office. They step into the room, and their eyes fall on Hector's lifeless body, hanging ominously in the dim light. They both lift Hector off the hook to release his body.

Chapter 33
Serious Talk

The next day, a light gray SUV pulls up to a modest house. The driver steps out, circling around to open the passenger-side door. Tomas emerges, his face bruised and body temporarily crippled but clouded with concern. He strides toward the front door. He knocks firmly.

The door opens, revealing an older, short Hispanic woman with eyes filled with water. It's Rosa's mom, clearly restraining herself from releasing the flood of emotions. She looks up at Tomas briefly, then steps aside, silently motioning for him to come in.

Without a word, she gestures toward the back of the house and lowers her head, avoiding his gaze. Tomas moves toward the back, his steps heavy. He slides open the glass door and steps outside.

Rosa's mom moves to the kitchen, looking out the back window to witness what's about to unfold in the yard. Tiffany is playing. She spots Tomas, freezes, and then runs to him with an eager expression.

Tomas bends down, taking her hand gently. He looks at her, and she looks right back with such innocence. Without speaking, he leads her to a pair of chairs nearby. They sit, and for a moment, he watches her face, trying to find the right words.

Then, in a soft, somber voice, each word weighted down with sorrow and a heavy heart, Tomas tells Tiffany what happened to Rosa.

The End...Family scars run deep.

About the Author

Producer Larry Love is a visionary storyteller with a knack for captivating audiences across multiple creative platforms. With a dynamic career spanning film, music, and now literature, Producer Larry Love has established himself as a creative force dedicated to pushing boundaries and telling stories that resonate deeply with people.

Now, venturing into the literary arena, Producer Larry Love brings his passion to the pages with his debut book, *Scar 2.0: Family Scars Run Deep*. This gritty, suspenseful novel that's receiving rave reviews explores themes of ethics, legacy, the cost to rise to power, and invites readers to immerse themselves in a gripping narrative full of twists, complex characters, and high-stakes drama that once again shows Larry's talented creativity. "It's a story of ambition and struggles. *Scar 2.0* tells the journey of Tomas Montgomery, who is given the chance to gain wealth and power through illegal means. This odyssey is about searching the human heart and questioning moral dilemmas." Larry states.

With Larry's diverse creative background and commitment to excellence, it will promise an unforgettable experience in *Scar 2.0*. His journey from music, film, and now literature is a testament to his ambition and artistry, making him someone to watch. Whether you're a fan of bold narratives, heart-pounding suspense, or thought-provoking themes, Producer Larry Love delivers a tale that will leave you wanting more.

Discover his latest work and join him on this thrilling new chapter of his creative journey!

Read more at thescar2.com.

www.ingramcontent.com/pod-product-compliance
Lightning Source LLC
Chambersburg PA
CBHW052058270326
41931CB00012B/2801